D0153874

Caring and Socia

Caring and Social Justice

Marian Barnes

palgrave
macmillan

First published 2006 by
PALGRAVE MACMILLAN
Houndmills, Basingstoke, Hampshire RG21 6XS and
175 Fifth Avenue, New York, N.Y. 10010
Companies and representatives throughout the world

PALGRAVE MACMILLAN is the global academic imprint of the Palgrave Macmillan division of St. Martin's Press, LLC and of Palgrave Macmillan Ltd. Macmillan® is a registered trademark in the United States, United Kingdom and other countries. Palgrave is a registered trademark in the European Union and other countries.

ISBN-13: 978–1–4039–2161–1   hardback
ISBN-10: 1–4039–2161–X   hardback
ISBN-13: 978–1–4039–2162–8   paperback
ISBN-10: 1–4039–2162–8   paperback

This book is printed on paper suitable for recycling and made from fully managed and sustained forest sources.

A catalogue record for this book is available from the British Library.

A catalog record for this book is available from the Library of Congress.

10   9   8   7   6   5   4   3   2   1
15   14   13   12   11   10   09   08   07   06

Printed in China

3/19/07

For Mum, Win Barnes (1913–2000)

Contents

Preface

My aim in this book is to offer an alternative way of viewing care-giving to that evident in much of the substantial literature that exists on this subject. This is intended to encourage a social care practice capable of supporting caring relationships so that the value and integrity of individual care givers and receivers is respected. This should take place within the context of social policies which recognise the contribution that care-giving can make to social cohesion and social justice.

The overwhelming emphasis of much of the existing body of work on caring is to present care-giving as a *problem*: for those giving and receiving care, as an expression of gendered social relations, as contributing to the oppression of disabled and older people, and for policy makers and practitioners seeking to minimise demands on the welfare state. One effect of this, I argue, is that front-line practitioners adopt a very narrow perspective in assessing and responding to the needs of those involved in caring relationships. They focus on the immediate situation rather than viewing this in the context of shared biographies, and their responses seek to balance assessment of risk with levels of dependency rather than offering help to support the achievement of aspirations. As a result, carers often experience such interventions as unhelpful or as missing the point. When presenting my ideas for this project to a carers' organisation I received consider-able support for the approach advocated here and a great willingness to support a project that aimed to contribute to the development of more holistic and effective practice.

At a social level a care perspective alerts us to the inadequacy of notions of social justice located solely in appeals to individual rights. In line with Tronto (1993), in an analysis developed by Sevenhuijsen (1998), I argue that a broad conception of social justice requires the inclusion of the principles of attentiveness, reciprocity, responsibility, competence and responsiveness which have been defined as constituting an 'ethic of

care'. At a collective level: 'Solidarity without care leads to an impov-
erished sense of morality and collective responsibility, because it can
only recognize others if they are "like us" or needy, pathetic, pitiful
and worthy of "our" commiseration because of their comparative
deprivation in relation to "ourselves" ' (Sevenhuijsen, 1998, p. 147).

Starting with individual carers' stories and thus prioritising the
value of an understanding based in the subjective experience of
carers, the book develops this analysis in order to suggest ways in
which social care practitioners might more effectively seek to support
caring relationships in ways that neither sanctify carers nor assume
they are resources to be used or commanded (Twigg and Atkin, 1994).
I argue that such a practice is less likely to approach recipients of care
as the source of burden, or as individuals whose rights should be
championed in opposition to those of carers. Whilst the book starts
with individual stories, it also considers the significance of the carers'
movement as one example of a range of social movements in social
care which challenge dominant assumptions of expertise associated
with professional training and qualification, and draw our attention to
the importance of values in social relations. User and carer movements pose questions about the way in which we live together and how
we regard our fellow citizens. But this discussion also addresses the
tensions that have been created as a result of naming carers as a
distinct social group, at the same time as reflecting on the importance
of the movement in drawing attention to the significance of care and
caring relationships as a necessary aspect of social well-being.

The book draws on a range of sources, but the primary original
source is narrative interviews carried out with 12 carers. All the carers
involved were family members who constitute the majority of care-
givers. All but two had identified themselves as 'carers' through
becoming involved in a carers' organisation. One exception was a man
who was known to me as someone who had worked in paid caring
posts as well as having looked after his mother, and another man looking after his wife was identified by another of my interviewees. The
carers I interviewed offered to speak to me after I had explained the
purpose of this project to them and what it would involve for them.
Initially two other men had offered to talk to me but each subsequently
withdrew (in different ways). Thus ten of the twelve carers interviewed
were women. One was Asian, one Jamaican, one born in Ireland, one
in Germany and another from a Polish background. They were
involved in a range of current and former caring relationships,

although none was a child supporting an adult. Whilst it was important for the purpose of this book to include a range of experiences amongst the stories I generated, my intention was not to design research that aimed to access a 'representative' group of carers.

I argue the importance of narrative as a method – in working with carers and those they help, to make sense of their lives together and separately, and to imagine possible futures, and in the context of 'assessment' – a process I conceptualise as seeking sufficient understanding of others' lives in order to work with them to determine appropriate, 'helpful' (Shakespeare, 2000) interventions, and as a means of generating theories which can offer useful insights into the social role of care.

The book also draws from literature on care-giving from different nations and cultures not only to locate individual caring biographies within what Chamberlayne and King (2000) have called 'Cultures of Care', but also to reflect on different ways of viewing care from that which is most evident in the literature of white, Western cultures. For example, I will reflect on hooks' (1984) critique of white feminist analyses of motherhood and caring which points to a way of constructing care as part of a process through which people can challenge oppressions through solidarity in kinship groups. I will also consider the role of lay care in sustaining community in adversity – reflecting, for example, on the impact of HIV/AIDS on communities in southern Africa.

The book starts with a review of the main literature on caring. Whilst this is primarily empirical literature, there have been some conceptual, theoretical and critical analyses of care-giving and its place within both social policy and social relations, and recent work has given greater emphasis to this. I shall introduce some of this work which will be developed later in the book as my own analysis proceeds.

In Chapter 2 I provide an account of the process of generating the narratives, and compare this with other work which has adopted a biographical or life story approach in the context of social welfare. I consider the role narrative has played in research, practice and advocacy in social welfare and what are the characteristics of a narrative approach to life stories. I argue that such an approach has considerable value not only in enhancing our understanding of care-giving and what this means, but also as a basis for developing a helpful practice to support both care-givers and care-receivers.

In Chapters 3 to 5 I introduce the stories told to me by the carers I interviewed. I describe how each person came to be involved in providing care through a temporal analysis of their narrative, and briefly summarise what we can learn from these stories about caring in the context of individual and shared lives.

In Chapter 6 I develop my analysis of carers' stories to consider what care-giving means to the 12 carers whose stories I have told. I introduce the concept of an 'ethic of care' and suggest how this can inform an understanding of the moral dilemmas with which individual care-givers are faced, and can start to enable us to consider the relationship between care-giving and social justice. Chapter 7 discusses the involvement of these 12 carers in carers' groups and other action intended to raise the profile of care and caring in policy making. It considers the contribution made by the carers' movement to understanding the nature of caring relationships and to the broader significance of care as a social good. I also consider the impact of the carers' movement in the context of other user movements on social work and social care policy and practice.

Chapter 8 develops the analysis of the previous two chapters to draw out the broader social and political implications of an ethic of care perspective to an understanding of the relationship between caring and social justice. Chapter 9 addresses the nature of social care practices capable of embodying both care and justice, and sensitive to the circumstances and histories of particular caring relationships. The chapter develops and integrates the narrative and ethic of care approaches and concludes with a brief discussion of a new imaginary of care to underpin future policy.

Acknowledgements

This book would not have been possible without the preparedness of twelve people to talk with me about their lives, including both the joys and struggles of caring. They were hugely generous with their time and with the very personal experiences they spoke to me about. Their names and the names of those they care for have been changed in this text, but you know who you are. I hope the result will do justice to what you have told me and to why you agreed to speak to me.

A modified version of Chapter 1 can be found in *Labour and Informality: Rethinking Ideas of Work*, edited by Martha Chen, Sukti Dasgupta, Renana Jhabvalala and Guy Standing, Geneva: ILO, forthcoming.

CHAPTER 1

Perspectives on Care and Care-Giving

Family members, friends and neighbours have always looked after people who are old, frail, sick or disabled. But it was only in the final twenty years of the twentieth century that such care-giving came to be named, identified as an issue for social policy and service providers, and that the experience of care-giving became the subject of empirical research and academic study. The term 'carer' was not formally recognised until the early 1980s in the United Kingdom (UK) and still has no distinct identity in many languages apart from English. In Italian, for example, the word is not recognised, and those who in England might be termed carers are usually identified as 'family members'. Research on the subject is rare (Taccani, 1994). This is significant. In this book I argue that the identification and naming of carers as a distinct social group has had an important impact in terms of policy, practice, theory and ethics issues, but that it has also created difficulties and dilemmas in each of these areas. I will discuss these dilemmas and offer both practical and conceptual ways to address them.

In this chapter I start with a perspective on the literature on caring that has both accompanied and contributed to the emergence of caring as a significant issue for social policy and practice. Others have undertaken similar reviews at different times over the last twenty years (for example, Parker 1985; Twigg *et al.*, 1990; Stalker, 2003) and each has adopted a rather different way of summarising existing research and knowledge for the particular purpose being pursued. My analysis is designed to provide a starting point from which my arguments concerning the embeddedness of caring within particular relationships can be developed, and from which I can explore the broader role of caring in the context of social justice and well-being.

Who cares and for whom do they care?

Responsibility for the nurturing and socialisation of children is a key purpose and responsibility of parents. In different cultures and at different times those responsibilities have been shared with other community members on both formal and informal bases. Examples include shared responsibilities for child care in Israeli kibbutzim, the role of 'othermothers' and grandmothers amongst black communities in Africa and in the black diaspora (S.M. James, 1993; Gibson, 2002), the provision of education and care in *balwadis* run by women's voluntary organisations in India (Caplan, 1985), and the range of supports, both paid and unpaid, provided between families throughout the world to substitute care to assist women to work for pay (for example, Mayall and Petrie, 1977; Leira, 1990). But the concept of parental care for offspring is familiar and well accepted.

Family responsibilities for the care of disabled, ill or frail older relatives are more contested and are evolving in line with changes in demography and health profiles. The impacts of these changes are rather different in different parts of the world. In the UK, women who had given up paid work to look after elderly parents first identified themselves as a distinctive group in the 1950s. In 1981 the first organisation was formed using the term 'carers' to include anyone providing unpaid care for elderly or disabled friends or relatives (M. Barnes, 1997a). The identification of a category of carer distinct from other familial relationships evidenced a growing awareness of new types of family structures and an expansion of the contexts within which quite considerable levels of support were being provided within kinship groups. One factor influencing this is the changing age structure of the population. In the developed world there has been a substantial increase in the numbers and proportion of older people in the population. In 2001 in the UK, 15.6 per cent of the population were aged 65 and over. This compares with 10.8 per cent fifty years earlier. The percentage is projected to increase to 24.3 per cent – virtually one-quarter of the population – by 2051 (ONS, 1998). Similar increases are predicted in other Western countries. Of particular relevance to the impact of an ageing population on the extent of lay care is the number of very old people. In Europe as a whole the population of those aged 80 and over is projected to increase 2.15 times between 1980 and 2025, from 11 million to 23.7 million (Dooghe, 1992).

Within developing countries, population structures are very different, although there is some indication that numbers and proportions of older people are also increasing in those societies. For example, Borj (2001) reported that the proportion of people 60 years and over in Brazil increased from 4 per cent in 1940 to 8 per cent in 1996. In China the 1990 census showed those over 60 comprised 8.6 per cent of the population, with this percentage predicted to rise to 20 per cent by 2025, with the proportion of older people in the population rising more quickly in urban areas (Harper, 1992). In India, although only 4 per cent of the population were aged over 65 in 2001, a decline in fertility rates and an increase in life expectancy means that reference is starting to be made to an 'ageing population'.

Whilst old age does not necessarily imply frailty or poor health, the increase in survival rates has resulted in a situation in which adult children more often find themselves looking after elderly parents, and elderly spouses may find themselves involved in rather different types of marital or partner relationships towards the end of their lives. As well as improved health care and living conditions contributing to a rise in the numbers and proportions of older people, these improvements have also resulted in larger numbers of disabled and chronically ill people surviving at all ages. Thus parents may be involved in the care of disabled children beyond the time when they would usually have expected such children to be independent, and friends, lovers and neighbours may be providing support for disabled or ill contemporaries. Disabled adults often become parents and this has led to a situation in which an increasing number of children in European countries are providing support to their parents, over and above that which might be expected in relation to able-bodied parents (Aldridge and Becker, 1994; Becker, 1995).

At the same time, what appear to be 'new' health problems have created new groups of people needing support. Within the UK the appearance of variant Creutzfeldt-Jakob disease (CJD) as an outcome of BSE (bovine spongiform encephalopathy) in cows has resulted in a small but intensive increase in the level of care provided within families (Myles et al., 2002). The emergence of AIDS (aquired immune deficiency syndrome) has resulted not only in different groups within the population needing support – in the West, often young and comparatively affluent people with HIV (human immuno-deficiency virus) or AIDS; in Southern Africa, children orphaned by the death of parents from AIDS – but also what may be regarded as 'non-traditional' carers finding themselves in this role. As Altman writes:

> Unlike other diseases with which such countries need contend, AIDS threatens above all the young and the healthy; that it is predominantly a sexually transmitted disease means that most of its direct victims are aged 15–45, so that the indirect victims of this epidemic include millions of children and other dependants of the formerly young and healthy. (1994, p.1)

In the West, young partners and other friends, as well as families, support the sufferers themselves, and there are carers' support groups specifically for those who care for someone with HIV/AIDS. In southern Africa care for orphaned children is often taken on by grandparents. The significance of this is not only that older people are providing care to younger family members, but they themselves are not receiving the financial and other support which they might have expected in their old age. Moller (quoted in Warnes, 1997) notes that the majority of black older people in South Africa live with children and grandchildren. Desmond *et al.* (n.d.) report evidence of decreases in material resources in households where there has been an adult AIDS death, as well as an increase in the percentage of elderly people in such households. Support is available from extended families and communities, but as Desmond *et al.* note: 'it remains unknown whether families and communities will be able to provide assistance to the sheer numbers of orphans in the near future' (p.19).

These changes have resulted in a situation in which the significance of 'care' in the context of the ordinary lives of families throughout the world is extending well beyond the care provided by parents for children until they become independent. In the UK, 17 per cent of households have a carer (Department of Health, 1999). The circumstances and life stages of those providing care to family members and friends is more diverse now than it has ever been. The provision of care crosses generations in more than one direction and can be both more complex and longer term than was formerly the case (Clarke, 1995).

In the UK and other parts of the developed world, commentators have compared the impact of demographic shifts leading to an increase in the numbers of people needing care and support with other social changes which cast doubt on the 'availability' of 'traditional' carers – adult women. Elsewhere other social and economic changes are cited as adversely affecting the 'availability' of lay carers. For example, Sambasivan (2001) refers to an increase in migration of Indian software professionals to the United States, Europe and Australia, leaving their elderly parents to have recourse to paid care – or to migrate to the country where their children now live. The issue of 'transnational care' – immigrant workers, often poorly paid, sometimes illegal, who provide care for more affluent families – has been recognised and is being researched (Hondagneu-Sotelo, 2000; Ehrenreich and Hochschild, 2003). Suggestions that an increase in the availability of support from state services will cause family members to withdraw their support have not been supported by research evidence (Lingsom, 1997; Penning, 2002). And evidence from research into the experiences of carers has revealed that concern about the quality of public services is one factor influencing motivations to care (Nolan *et al.*, 1996).

Estimates of the numbers of carers depend on the way in which 'carer' is defined – by researchers or subjectively (Fisher, 1997). Analysis of the British Household Surveys of 1985, 1990 and 1995 indicates an increase in the number of adults identifying themselves as carers from 1985 to 1990, but with numbers dropping back again in 1995 (Hirst, 2001) – probably because of a tightening of the definition used. Secondary analysis of the British Household Panel Survey between 1991 and 1998 reveals a slight decrease in the overall prevalence of extra-resident care provided by women, but no significant change in the prevalence of co-resident care by women. There was an increase of approximately 3 per cent per year in co-resident care-giving by men. The trends indicate a decline in care-giving between households and an increase in care-giving within households. Dooghe (1992) reviews a range of studies of lay caring in a number of countries which confirmed the predominance of women carers and the significant proportion of carers who were themselves elderly.

During the 1990s in the UK, attention was drawn to the situation of carers in minority ethnic communities (for example, Atkin and Rollings, 1992; Walker and Ahmad, 1994; Chamba *et al.*, 1999). Whilst they share many of the demographic characteristics of white carers in the UK, researchers have concluded that experiences are made more difficult by racism and inappropriate assumptions about the nature of family relationships within different ethnic communities.

What is care?

The emergence of 'care' as an issue for public services and public policies in Western societies has led to diverse attempts to describe, classify and conceptualise what precisely 'care' consists of.

Caring activities

Research has generated descriptions of the range and intensity of tasks undertaken by carers in different circumstances (for example, Lewis and Meredith, 1988; G. Parker, 1993). These include washing, feeding, getting in and out of bed, assistance with toileting, giving medication, changing dressings, giving injections or catheterisation, dealing with incontinence, assistance with paperwork and personal business including managing money, negotiation and liaison with 'professional' caring agencies and staff, providing transport and undertaking household tasks.

Some of these activities overlap with and may be indistinguishable from activities undertaken by trained professionals and other care workers (Traustadottir, 2000). Pickard and Glendinning (2002) have looked at the similarities between the tasks undertaken by carers of elderly people and those carried out by nurses. However, whilst there is in some cases a considerable overlap in the content of these tasks, the context within which tasks are carried out means that the nature of the relationship is very different from that with professional care-givers such as nurses. Other types of task are those that are more usually associated with child care and have led to some carers experiencing caring as a form of role reversal (in the case of children providing care to parents), or as transforming one type of relationship into another: 'Well, instead of being like partners or husband and wife, I feel like I'm a mother looking after a child' (Pickard and Glendinning, 2002, p. 148). Other tasks involve more administrative or organisational skills. Nicky James (1992) describes this as follows:

> The domestic carer can be characterised as being responsible both for overall organisation, and for the details of an individual's care. The person cared for may be able to negotiate their requirements – even if it is displayed by throwing food they do not like back at the carer – but responsibility for planning the menus, shopping, cooking, cleaning and co-ordinating this with other requirements remains with the carer. (p. 494)

We can add to this list responsibilities for ensuring co-ordination between lay and paid care where this is provided, co-ordinating support from other members of the family or from friends, and negotiating the use of their own time between caring responsibilities and looking after other family members (for example, their own children as well as elderly parents), and/or paid work.

The range, intensity and mix of caring activities relate both to circumstances of the person receiving care, and to the availability of formal care services, as well as being mediated by gender and the nature of the relationship between care-giver and care-receiver. For example, intimate care is rarely provided by male carers and it is not always the case that intimate personal relationships (for example, between spouses and partners) mean that intimate care is provided within those relationships (Ungerson, 1987; Twigg and Atkin, 1994).

An emphasis on the tasks of caring, their range, intensity and the physical demands they can place on carers, together with the emotional impact of caring and the impact caring can have on the capacity of carers to undertake paid work and have a 'life of their own', has led to much of the emphasis in caring research to focus on the 'burden' of care (for example, Bayley, 1973; Briggs and Oliver, 1985; Levin, Sinclair and Gorbach, 1989; Braithwaite, 1990).

Labour and emotion in context

Conceptualisations of care have distinguished the affective and practical dimensions of caring: 'caring about' and 'tending' (R. Parker, 1981). 'Caring about' or concern for another person can be expressed in a number of ways. It can be expressed through the way in which physical care is provided, but it can also be expressed and delivered through spending time with someone, holding hands, stroking his or her hair, or giving gifts. It would be wrong to suggest that the distinction between caring for and tending necessarily describes the difference between paid care and that provided within family, friendship or other personal relationships (Warren, 1990; Stone, 2000; Traustadottir, 2000). As these authors and Twigg (2000) have demonstrated, paid carers working in front-line jobs providing domestic and personal care can develop attachments to their 'clients', demonstrated in some cases by a preparedness to go beyond their paid duties in the provision of support, as well as in the concern they demonstrate whilst carrying out their duties. In contrast, evidence of abuse within familial 'caring relationships' also demonstrates that it can be hard to sustain concern for the person to whom care is being provided in some circumstances (Pillemer and Kinkelhor, 1988; Ogg and Bennett, 1992). However, within Western societies the source of care-giving within families and amongst friends is usually a mixture of love, obligation, duty and reciprocity, and some affective content is a key dimension of lay care (Ungerson, 1987; Qureshi and Walker, 1989; Finch and Mason, 1993).

Detailed comparative research would be needed to confirm the universality of care-giving motivations. A study of care-giving in rural Arab communities in Israel identified one response to the issue of determining who should provide care that seemed to have little to do with the emotional content of family relationships. In describing a 'unilateral-decision style', Katz and Lowenstein (2002) quote an 82-year-old man talking about how caring tasks were allocated after his return from hospital following an amputation:

> I decided upon my return from the hospital that my personal care will be given by my wife, household chores will be done by my three daughters and available daughters-in-law, and shopping and the contacts with the health clinic will be the responsibility of my two sons. (p. 68)

Another perspective on this, which draws from the work of Philip Abrams (1978) may be less culturally specific. As a result of his empirical studies of care-giving, Abrams suggested that a key characteristic of this is that such care is '*personally directed*: given to people by virtue of their pre-established relationships, and not therefore available to others in similar need' (Qureshi and Walker, 1989, p. 146, my emphasis). Not only is lay care only available to people with whom a relationship already exists, an important motivation is that it is particular and designed for that person rather than the impersonal care available to all who meet specified criteria, which is provided through the state, or to those who can pay the relevant charges to purchase private services. This is evident in a number of different contexts. In her study of African American women caring for grandchildren, Gibson (2002) identified a number of dimensions to a general theme of 'relationships with grandchildren' as being significant in their explanations of why they took on this care. These included both keeping grandchildren out of the care of strangers and seeing care-giving as contributing to the future generation.

Concerns with the future are less significant in the context of adult children caring for elderly parents, but the importance of personalised care rather than care by strangers is a theme in many studies of caring in these contexts (for example, Lewis and Meredith, 1988; Twigg and Atkin, 1994). Pickard and Glendinning (2002) and M. Barnes (1996) highlight the significance of the particular type of expertise carers develop. This does not derive from formal training and is not based in generalisable knowledge about particular 'conditions' and the type of support needs to which these may give rise. Rather it is knowledge based in intimate and exclusive understanding of a particular person, gained from intensive interaction with that person on a daily basis.

But these particular relationships also need to be understood within a broader social context. The study of care-giving in rural Arab communities in Israel suggests that the social, economic and political processes leading to change in what Katz and Lowenstein describe as a 'society in transition' have impacted on the way in which families adapt to chronic illness and subsequent care-giving. They suggest that the more adaptive and flexible families, that is, those less traditional in their outlook, experienced less burden and more satisfaction in caring. Sambasivan (2001) however, cautions that the growth of individualisation that is part of a process of 'development' is in danger of undermining the 'familial self' and posing a threat to the care of elderly people.

Lay care-giving is thus embedded within particular relationships and within both individual and shared biographies, which are themselves embedded within different cultural contexts and welfare systems (Chamberlayne and King, 2000). Unlike relationships which may develop between paid care-givers and those they support which may come to include a significant affective content, these relationships have a history that affects the response of both care-provider and -receiver to the new situation in which they find themselves. But the process of decision making about 'who cares' is not solely a matter of personal choice based only on affective relationships. It is the result of both implicit and explicit negotiations within families and amongst other close relations (Finch and Mason, 1993), and influenced by the policies of state welfare systems and the availability and quality of public services (for example, Lewis, 1998; Harrington Meyer and Kersterke Storbakken, 2000; Daly, 2001).

Care as work

Building on the analysis of the tasks and activities of caring, and the affective dimension of this, Nicky James (1992) has defined caring in terms of three types of work: physical labour, emotional labour and organisational labour. The term 'emotional labour' was first coined by Hochschild (1983) in the context of a study of the work of flight attendants and has subsequently been used to understand the nature of many types of work, not only that undertaken by lay or professional carers. It refers to the way in which people manage their own emotions in order to influence the feelings of others. Care needs to be 'organised' in relation to the everyday needs of the person receiving support, the input provided by paid carers and in relation to the other responsibilities and needs of the carer. The physical tasks of caring are perhaps the most visible dimension of care as they respond to the basic human requirements of eating, sleeping, bathing/washing, dressing/undressing, defecating and urinating. Emotional labour is integrated into the way in which tending care is given and received on a day-to-day basis, but may also be required in response to major life crises – for example, in supporting someone making decisions about treatment for life-threatening diseases or about whether to move from their own home into residential care.

More recently Twigg (2000) has discussed care as 'bodywork': 'Bodywork involves working directly on the bodies of others... Typically it involves touching, manipulating and assessing the bodies of others, which thus become the objects of the workers' labour' (p. 137). Whilst her main focus is on front-line workers employed to carry out personal care, her focus on the neglected aspects of the bodily dimension of care is also relevant to an understanding of the different types of work involved in care-giving by lay carers. It adds another dimension to an understanding of the physicality of care-giving.

This characterisation of care as work of different types is the result of analysis by researchers. It is not evident that carers themselves view care in the same way as they view 'work', although they do emphasise the substantial demands that providing care can make. Ungerson (1987) suggests that there may be a gender dimension to the way in which carers themselves conceptualise care-giving. She suggests male carers may be more likely than female carers to make sense of their roles by conceptualising care as work. She describes how husbands caring for their wives drew from their experience of paid work to organise the process of care-giving and to 'manage' their wives. She also highlights the professional language which one man in particular utilised to describe his wife and other carers: 'a carer must be in charge. I see some of my *colleagues* there [at a Carers' Support Group] – they're completely under the thumb of their *invalid patient*' (p. 107).

One observation which is frequently made by carers is that caregiving, whether described as a task or job or in any other way, is not confined to specified working hours. Carers are 'on duty' 24 hours a day, 7 days a week, unless they get a break through the provision of respite services, or by someone taking over on an informal basis. As Pickard and Glendinning describe this, caring 'is boundless: it is not contained within a specific timescale, but is virtually limitless, characterised by spontaneous, unexpected events or crises which could occur at any time, with demands being made during the night experienced as particularly onerous' (2002, p.148).

Both the physical and emotional dimensions of caring can have adverse consequences for carers. For example, dealing with incontinence can be both stressful and embarrassing; behavioural and interpersonal problems which can be associated with dementia, learning difficulties and mental health problems can cause considerable anxiety, stress and pain; the knowledge of inevitable deterioration until death associated with dementia and degenerative physical conditions is hard to bear; whilst the physical work involved in lifting someone in and out of bed, doing daily laundry as well as regular housework is not only stressful, but can cause considerable health problems for carers (for example, Braithwaite, 1990; Twigg and Atkin, 1994).

But whilst caring is often experienced as demanding, carers do not necessarily experience or describe caring as a 'burden'. Caring can also be a source of satisfaction – what Nolan *et al.* (1996) describe as the 'neglected dimension' of caring. Those satisfactions can also lead to benefits or rewards, including offering a sense of purpose and value in life, and an identity. In this way caring can serve similar functions to paid work for individual carers. Whilst Nolan *et al.* suggest that there are circumstances in which the satisfactions of caring can bind people into situations which perhaps should not be sustained, they conclude that 'these concerns are outweighed by the potential for the satisfactions of caring to be used in a number of positive ways to assist carers and cared-for persons achieve a better quality of life' (p. 103).

Typologies of care

Bowers (1987) sought to distinguish different types of care provided by adult children caring for parents with dementia. Nolan *et al.* (1996) have developed her typology to propose a way of categorising the care that might be provided in a range of different circumstances. They distinguish: anticipatory care; preventive care; supervisory care; instrumental care; protective care; preservative care; (re)constructive care; and reciprocal care (p. 39). It is instrumental care which has received most attention in research into caring, but this more sophisticated analysis extends an understanding of the concept and practice of caring into areas which Bowers argued had previously been 'invisible'. These include action taken well before actual help is required and not revealed to the person who is the focus of attention. Such actions that anticipate deterioration in the individual's condition can have a profound effect on the carer's life. One example of anticipatory care is a decision to move house to be closer to elderly parents in order to be 'on hand' if the need arises.

(Re)constructive care looks forward in a rather different way. One impact of chronic illness or disability can be to make it difficult or impossible to sustain former interests and activities which have been an important part of a person's identity.

The purpose of (re)constructive care is to build on the past in order to develop new and valued roles. We have named it *(re)constructive* care in recognition of the differences that are apparent in certain caring relationships. Parents of children with learning difficulties, for example, are more likely to engage in *constructive* care in order to build an identity and a set of roles for their child. On the other hand, carers of either spouses or parents are more likely to engage in *reconstructive* care where the purpose is to rebuild an identity on the foundations of past histories and biographies. (Nolan *et al.*, 1996, pp. 44–5).

In addition to these different ways in which caring has been conceptualised, there are also a variety of ways of defining the *care-giver*. These have changed over time, but also reflect something of their origins and the purpose for which they were developed. For example, the Equal Opportunities Commission (EOC) in the UK came up with a broad and relatively unsophisticated definition in the context of a report arguing for the support needs of carers themselves to be recognised: '[a]nyone who looks after or cares for a handicapped person to any extent in their own home or elsewhere' (EOC, 1982). Researchers have adopted particular definitions for the purposes of addressing specific questions in relation to care and caring. One example is the definition used by Braithwaite in an Australian study designed to explore what contributes to care-giving being experienced as a burden: 'People who assume the major responsibility for providing caregiving services on a regular basis to someone who is incapable of providing for him/herself' (Braithwaite, 1990). A UK guide for social services practitioners undertaking assessments of people seeking help from local Social Services departments includes a comment about the type of 'dependency relationship' involved in its definition of a carer:

A person who is not employed to provide the care in question by anybody in the exercise of its function under any enactment. Normally, this will be a person who is looking after another adult in the home who is frail, ill and/or mentally or physically disabled, and where the dependency relationship exceeds that implicit in normally dependent relationships between family members. (Social Services Inspectorate, 1991).

What is common about these, and most other, definitions is that they emphasise caring as a practical, instrumental activity, undertaken in relation to another person who is unable to carry out those activities for themselves.

Critiques of 'care'

The gendered nature of care-giving led to significant feminist critiques of policies and practices which assumed that women could and should provide the main source of support to family members (for example, Finch and Groves, 1983; Finch, 1984; Dalley, 1988; Lewis, 1998; Harrington Meyer, 2000). These perspectives were, in turn subject to critique by disabled feminists and other disabled activists (for example, Morris, 1995). The notion of care as an appropriate designation of the support needed by disabled people is disputed because of the way in which this constructs disabled people as dependent and passive. The dependency-inducing notion of care is contrasted with rights to the support necessary to enable disabled people live their lives in the way that they want (C. Barnes, 1991). Shakespeare (2000) has argued for an approach to such support based on the notion of 'helpfulness', suggesting that the concept of help may be a more useful basis for understanding the importance of support which does not imply passivity or dependency.

One of the key practical implications of such critiques has been the development of direct payments designed to give disabled people control over the help they receive. In the UK and some other European countries (for example, Holland, Sweden, Germany, France and Denmark) disabled people can receive financial payment to buy their own support services (Glasby and Littlechild, 2002). One consequence of this is that they become employers of their own personal assistants (PAs). When a Direct Payments scheme was first introduced (on a voluntary basis) in England and Wales in 1996, payments could not be used to pay a family member to act as a PA. This was cited as one reason for the slow implementation of the Direct Payments scheme in many areas (Witcher *et al.*, 2000). In Sweden, in comparison, disabled people have had a right to direct payments with the option of employing a family member in this capacity since 1994. Similarly in California a programme called 'In-Home Supportive Services' enables disabled people to employ a family member or other person to provide personal assistance with the cost of this met by the state. Under this scheme, 47 per cent of consumers hire a relative and another 25 per cent someone other than a relative whom they already knew (Walsh, 2001).

Concerns have been expressed about direct payment schemes in relation to the way in which PAs may be treated by people who are likely to be inexperienced as employers (Pijl, 2000). Ungerson (1997) has also expressed misgivings about the scheme from this perspective in an article which received considerable criticism from within the disability movement. In this context the Direct Payments scheme is different from previous schemes which enabled payments to be made to lay carers to support them in those roles (see for example, Qureshi *et al.*, 1983) which did not create an employer–employee relationship between care provider and recipient. But regardless of the effectiveness with which disabled people carry out their role as employers, the introduction of a financial payment to family care-givers is likely to have an impact on the nature of caring relationships. One potential effect is that the concept of care as work becomes strengthened, although Walsh's study of a process of unionising home care workers employed in the California scheme referred to above demonstrated that both the nature of caring work and the dispersed nature of the work environment meant that union organisers had to develop a 'worker consciousness' (2001, p. 223) in order to organise them.

In a rather different context Lund (1991, quoted in Mayo, 1994) notes the tensions that can emerge when people who are lay carers develop skills which lead to opportunities for paid employment. Describing a project designed to develop training materials and strengthen support structures for community-based lay carers of black elderly people in South Africa she writes:

> Both in this project and in the community health workers study, the situation has arisen where project leaders have frowned on the fact that women carers see this voluntary participation as possibly open-ing doors for jobs, through receiving skills training, making connec-tions, becoming visible outside the home. It is as if this motivation is seen by the (well-paid) leaders as betraying the notion of altruis-tic service to the community – wanting a job is somehow seen as greedy or selfish (quoted in Mayo, 1994, p. 198).

Caring and social well-being

The significance of lay care to the delivery of social welfare is explicit in the social policy discourses of welfare states. The normative accep-tance of the value of lay care is clearly evident in this extract from the Griffiths Report, a report commissioned by the British government and which was influential in determining government policy on community care embodied in the 1990 National Health Service and Community Care Act:

> Publicly provided services constitute only a small part of the total care provided to people in need. Families, friends, neighbours and other local people provide the majority of care in response to needs which they are uniquely well placed to identify and respond to. This will continue to be the primary means by which people are enabled to live normal lives in community settings. The proposals take as their starting point that this is as it should be, and that the first task

of publicly provided services is to support and where possible strengthen these networks of carers. (Griffiths, 1988, para 3.2).

More recently the New Labour Government of the UK produced a National Strategy for Carers (Department of Health, 1999). The introduction to this report continued the theme, making explicit not only the resource contribution made by lay carers to the state, but also the significance of caring at the level of communities:

> One in eight people in Britain is now a carer – looking after some-one who is ill, frail, disabled or unable to cope. Without this exten-sive caring, many more elderly, frail, sick or disabled people would need the support of statutory services, and might need to enter a residential or nursing home or go into hospital. This might be a detriment to the quality of life for some people needing care, and would be at considerable cost to the taxpayer. In communities, the networks of giving, or caring, and of supporting relatives, friends and neighbours are part of the glue that helps join society together. (p. 11)

Most research on the subject of lay care focuses on the significance of care in the context of interpersonal relationships – within the context of the individual support needed by disabled, ill or frail people of all ages if they are to remain living in their own homes. However, the quotation from *Caring About Carers* also suggests that lay care contributes to the capacity of states to meet the welfare needs of their citizens, and introduces the notion that lay care-giving needs to be understood in terms of a broader function than solely providing support for individuals – it also needs to be understood as a force for social cohesion.

This identification of a social as well as personal dimension of caring has led to analyses that have considered caring as a duty of citi-zenship (for example, Harris, 2002). Under New Labour, carers are identified as making a 'vital and valued contribution to the economic and moral good of the country' (p. 274) and the notion that individual carers should be supported to enable them to continue to provide care to elderly or disabled relatives which emerged in the UK community care reforms of the 1990s is extended to a recognition of what Harris calls a 'community-in-adversity' (p. 275).

Harris argues the need to be aware of the dangers of an over-emphasis on 'caring-as-citizenship-obligation' (p. 277). He suggests that this emphasises the notion of those receiving support as 'burdens', and cautions an over-idealization of the family as the most appropriate location for care of older people. But it *is* important to understand care in a wider context than simply what goes on within the private worlds of caring relationships. Discomfort with the notion that caring *should* be an *obligation* of citizenship is only one way of considering the place of caring in a social context. England *et al.* (unpublished paper quoted by Curran, 2002) have argued that care should be considered as a 'public good'. One condition of a public good concerns 'subtractability' – in this case that the removal of caring would harm all members of society. This is evident in the impact this would have on the cost of state substitution for lay care, and the personal costs to individuals. As the above discussion of the diverse nature of care indicates, these personal costs would not simply be loss of practical support, but also loss of emotional support and loss of the significant contributions care can make to self-esteem and sense of personal value – not only to the care recipient, but also in many instances to the carer.

Conclusions

The extensive literature on care and care-giving has made visible the extent and diversity of the work undertaken by family members and friends in supporting ill, frail, disabled or older people. It has revealed the particularity of care, its contextual nature and hence the differences as well as similarities between support provided by paid workers and by family members and friends. It has evidenced the gendered nature of care-giving, but also the increasing diversity of the circumstances in which care is given and received.

In addition to care as a distinctive type of work in the context of meeting the support needs of particular individuals, care has also been recognised as doing work for society and for community. From the perspective of the state it is an essential contribution to meeting the welfare needs of the population. One consequence of this is that caring has been expressed as a responsibility or even obligation in welfare discourse. There is often a fine line between policies designed to *support* lay care, and those that are effectively seeking to *command* such care.

In the remainder of the book I develop the connections between caring as the provision of direct support to specific individuals, and care as a social and political value, essential to the achievement of social justice.

CHAPTER 2

Telling Stories of Care-Giving: An Introduction to a Biographical Approach to Understanding Caring

As Chapter 1 has demonstrated, there is a substantial body of research on care and care-giving. Much of this research has focused on what constitutes care in terms of the work involved. This was intended to make visible the level of unpaid input being provided by family members in order to reveal the assumptions on which community care policy has been based. It has had a valuable impact both in the development of support services for carers, and in achieving recognition for the knowledge they bring. But it has also arguably contributed to the development of a 'them and us' position between carers and disabled people through positioning care receivers as 'dependent burdens' on carers, and constructing carers as 'tragic heroines' carrying the moral weight of society's obligations to its needy members. In this chapter I reflect on the value of adopting a life-story approach as a means of understanding the experience of caring in the context of individual and shared lives.

This approach is, in part, influenced by personal experience. My mother (a widow from 1973 until she died in 2000) lived the last ten or more years of her life with gradually developing dementia and in her final few years was on the receiving end of a package of care comprising input from home helps, attendance at a day centre (where she saw a psycho-geriatrician), occasional visits from CPNs (Community Psychiatric Nurses), and even more occasional visits from a social worker. My two elder sisters visited her regularly to provide company, some personal care, and help with shopping and collecting her pension. There was a rota for phoning her in the mornings to remind her when she was due to attend the day centre and to encourage her to do so – she was often reluctant about this. Their husbands also helped, for example, one would clean the house whilst my mother and sister went out shopping, and another on occasion dealt with emergency calls from neighbours or the home help. My third sister lives overseas and would visit Mum during her holidays for four or five days at a time. I visited at weekends (she lived three hours' drive from where I live) with the main emphasis on providing company and taking her to visit gardens and other places she enjoyed. Mum went to church most Sundays, and knitted blanket squares for Save the Children. In the earlier stages of her dementia she had continued attend a local history group, to work in a local Oxfam shop and to read for the Talking Book and Talking Newspaper services. She received very positive feedback from recipients of this in relation to the clarity of her voice and this was obviously very important for her.

My experience of the responses of paid workers involved in my mother's care was that their primary concern was the 'risk' she presented to herself and others because of her tendency to forget she had left saucepans on the gas cooker. They were also concerned about the appropriateness of her clothing for the weather and her somewhat dishevelled appearance. The primary concern for my sisters and me was my mother's unhappiness. My father's early death was a blow from which she never really recovered. As her dementia developed she was able neither to anticipate activities or visits, nor to remember them within hours of them having taken place. This was very evident when I returned home with her after her 80th birthday party, hosted by my eldest sister and attended by Mum's two remaining sisters, all her children and grandchildren and assorted nieces and nephews. Within an hour of our return home she asked me where we had had lunch that day. Hence her subjective experience of loneliness was probably more intense than the amount of contact she had might suggest. She spoke often of having had enough and wanting to die. Caring for her had a substantial emotional impact on all of us.

What upset me in particular about the response of paid workers was their apparent lack of interest in finding out about Mum as a person – what her life had been like, what her interests and skills were, what was important to her, and in trying to understand anything about the nature of her relationship with me and my sisters. She was summed up in the record of systematic reviews carried out at six-monthly intervals in the following kinds of way:

- Food – Does shopping but often multiple items, can still just about cook adequately. Regular checks to see that food is not 'going off'.
- Day-time activities – Not much but enjoys day care when she visits.
- Psychological distress – Often distressed and sometimes angry.
- Company – Lonely.

When I suggested during a case review meeting that it might be important to understand her reactions to her current situation by understanding a bit about her history and her former and current relationships with her daughters and other family members I got no response.

Biographical accounts, life histories and narratives are used in the context of both research and practice relating to social welfare in a number of different contexts, although, as this personal example illustrates, they are not necessarily a feature of social care assessments. Here I discuss some of the different purposes of such approaches, what are their key characteristics and how they can contribute to a better understanding of the lives and experiences of those who use health and social care services.

Life stories, family histories and narrative accounts

Researching

There has always been a tradition of narrative or biographical methods in social research, but this has often been neglected or devalued in favour of supposedly more rigorous 'scientific' approaches. Whilst research in this tradition focuses very immediately on the lived lives of particular individuals, this does not mean that it is only or primarily concerned with understanding those particular lives as discrete and separate. Indeed it has been claimed that: 'the maintenance of the fiction of the atomized individual becomes untenable with the adoption of a biographical perspective' (Miller, 2000, p. 2). Settersten (1999, p. 23) argues that life-course research must not only cover multiple domains, but also link these together, understanding individual development in the context of specific cohorts, ethnic groups, nation states and other social contexts. He suggests that too often researchers study lives as if they are independent of each other. Instead: 'We must begin to ask questions of our respondents meant to tap the interdependence of lives, capture those experiences from the vantage points of those involved, and unpack the nature, meanings and consequences of interdependence over time' (p. 15). Narrative and life-history research methods are concerned with understanding how the personal, the social, the economic, the political and the cultural are intertwined. They link macro and micro levels of analysis in order to reconnect with the realities of people's everyday lives at the same time as recognising how structural factors and historical events shape the possibilities that are open to individuals and provide the context within which individual agency may be exercised.

Biographical methods also link the present with the past and the future. They recognise that any evidence generated concerning the circumstances of those the research is about does not reflect a fixed state – those circumstances will probably change in the future and almost certainly were different in the past. This relates both to objective 'factual' evidence such as what job people may be doing, whether they have experienced any significant illness or disability, what is the composition of their family, and to subjective data: how people feel, what they think and how they make sense of things that are happening in their lives. People do not live solely in the present – who they are and how they live is affected by where they have come from and by their hopes, fears and anticipations of the future.

There is more than one type of approach to biographical or life-history research which Miller (2000) has argued correspond to three broad epistemological positions:

• Realist
• Neo-positivist, and
• Narrative

A researcher starting from a realist position would use life histories as a means of constructing general principles about social phenomena from the viewpoints of a number of different actors whose views are each taken to constitute an aspect of objective reality. Researchers working in the grounded theory tradition might adopt this approach. A neo-positivist would take a deductive approach, using pre-existing concepts and theoretical frameworks to make theoretically based predictions about people's experienced lives. In contrast, a narrativist places particular significance on how the story is generated. The emphasis is less on 'what happened' (although this is still important) but on what the telling reveals about the significance of events and experiences to the teller and how this can be interpreted. The context in which the story is generated is highly important because a research interview is understood not as a means of revealing pre-existing facts, but as an interaction through which a narrative is jointly generated.

Wengraf (2001) also distinguishes three purposes for research interviews of this type. We can use them to know about *discourse* – the way of talking adopted or chosen by the interviewee, which indicates deep-seated assumptions that determine what can and what cannot be said. For example, a psychiatrist is likely to speak about mental illness within a medical discourse that expresses certain assumptions about the origins of mental ill health and how it should be treated. In contrast, someone identifying themselves with the service user/survivor movement is unlikely to talk about their experiences in these terms. We can use interviews to uncover the *objective referents* – who did or said what, when and to whom. And we can use interviews to interpret something about the *subjectivity* of the interviewee: 'a model I construct of what I see as some of the permanent or transient characteristics of the subject who is acting as informant in the interview' (ibid., p. 9).

As both Miller and Wengraf note, these three different starting points or purposes rarely constitute a 'pure' or single approach to biographical interviewing. But the way in which any research project is designed will indicate which position constitutes the primary approach. For example, a narrativist will be interested in finding out what were the key events in people's lives, but will not design a highly structured large-scale survey to establish this. My approach in the interviews conducted for this book was primarily within the narrative tradition of life-story interviewing. Whilst I wanted to know in what circumstances people became carers and what caring consisted of in the different situations described, my primary purpose was to understand what caring meant to the carers I interviewed, how they made sense of their experience of care-giving in the context of other aspects of their lives and how they spoke about this – what did this reveal about notions of justice as well as what constituted care-giving from their perspective.

There are many examples of the use of biographical or life-story research being used in the context of social policy and social welfare. I will illustrate the varied contribution it can make with four examples.

A study by Bornat *et al.* (2000) illustrates how research into life changes and their impact on people virtually demands a biographical approach. The researchers were interested in the way in which family change – divorce, separation, and remarriage – impacts on older people and in how they are able both to accommodate such change within their own histories, as well as making sense of this through negotiating public discourses concerning personal morality and the 'death of the family'. The researchers' analysis revealed the importance to older people of maintaining identity and meaning in their lives and the strategies they used to develop a coherent biographical account of their lives and family histories. What became evident was not only the factual importance of coping with discontinuities in those histories, but also the way in which 'biographical work' was an important means to achieving this. Experiences which public discourses can associate with failure and which can thus be experienced with a sense of shame can impact negatively on an individual's concept of self. Finding some coherence and continuity within personal histories was necessary for the older people interviewed in order to prevent disruption within families having a damaging impact on themselves and their sense of family life.

Research using a biographical approach and which is directly relevant to the subject of this book is that by Chamberlayne and King (2000). Their study of care-giving in Britain and the two Germanies (West and East, after unification) was designed to understand how carers meet the challenge of the situation they find themselves in and how their personal responses to caring are interwoven with the different welfare regimes which define the policy context in which support for older and disabled people is provided. The study also aimed to identify the way in which 'cultures of care' emerge out of the interaction between private lives, the informal social networks through which people receive support, and the public resources and structures which constitute official policy and the services this delivers. Chamberlayne and King were able to distinguish different strategies developed by carers and suggested that these had a significant impact on their own lives and the lives of those they cared for. One strategy focused inward on the home and family, one outward and the third was 'torn' between the two. Such strategies are not *determined* by the public sphere of welfare, but do raise questions about how welfare regimes are able to respond to the very different situations of carers who retreat into the private sphere and seek resources and solutions within themselves, and those who are much more outward-looking and energetic in seeking solutions amongst social and public networks.

Booth and Booth's (1994) study of parents with learning difficulties was designed to enhance our understanding of a little-known experience and to contribute to the development of a practice which is more supportive of mothers, fathers and children in this position. The life story approach in this instance was explicitly intended to: 'give pride of place to the views of parents themselves and what they have to say about the rewards and demands of parenthood' (ibid., p. 1). It was developed in response to the limitations and inadequacies of the little research which previously existed on this subject and in the context of a growing body of research in which people with learning difficulties were informants. However, people with learning difficulties had rarely been involved in research which involved depth interviewing or a life story approach because of perceived limitations in their capacity to articulate their experiences and tell their story. Booth and Booth argued that a biographical method would have much to recommend it because it requires the researcher to 'listen to those who know' (p. 23) and access not only the subjective experiences of the interviewee, but through that to understand the structural features of their social world. Research of this type poses significant ethical issues and requires the development of trusting relationships between researcher and interviewees. But the book demonstrates both the potential of this method for enabling people with learning difficulties to tell their stories, and for the way in which this can lead to important insights not only for research but also for practice.

A much closer link between research and practice through the use of narrative and biographical approaches is illustrated by Kim Etherington's work with adult male survivors of child sexual abuse (Etherington, 2000). Etherington is a counsellor who also became a researcher. Her book tells a number of stories: of Mike and Stephen, two brothers who were sexually abused by their grandfather, of Etherington's counselling work with them, and of her journey as a researcher seeking to use the knowledge gained through this process as a means not only of communicating what it can tell us about the male experience of child sex abuse, but also what it can tell us about research understood as a process of dialogue between the researcher and those whose lives she is researching. Mike and Stephen tell their stories directly: through extracts from their diaries, through narrative accounts in which they recount what happened to them and how they felt about the abuse at the time it was happening and at the time they were receiving counselling, in poems and letters, and in extracts of conversations with their counsellor. Etherington adopts two identities: as counsellor she describes how she came to be involved with the two men and the nature of the relationship she established with them. She then discusses how story telling is used in counselling and how it can contribute to a process of healing:

> The past cannot be reinvented or changed, but through story telling we might shift the place our past takes in our present lives. Unassimilated fragments of our past haunt us in the present and we need to create closure of our past and continuity into the future; through narrative a sense of coherence can be restored. (p. 152)

As a researcher she adopts a fairly traditional structure for reporting how she went about the research, considering philosophical, ethical, data collection and analysis issues, but within this structure she describes her own journey putting together a 'bricolage' of research methods and approaches and her increasing comfort with the notion of the researcher's inclusion within the research. She also reproduces part of the transcript of conversations with Mike and Stephen where they discuss the difficult issues of anonymity when research tells individual stories in detail, as well as extracts from her own research diary.

Maintaining an identity

The brief review of the use of narrative and biographical approaches to research has demonstrated that such research can often have quite close links to practice. Whilst it is very important to be clear what is the nature of those links, and for researchers not to offer therapy unless research is an agreed element of a therapeutic process, the methods adopted within this type of research can be very similar to the methods used in other contexts and with other purposes. In some instances there is evidence that interviewees can gain direct benefit from the process of reflecting on their life stories. But it is also the case that this can be a distressing experience and there is no commitment in a research relationship to on-going contact to address any of the issues raised. Thus good practice requires researchers to indicate where such support can be obtained if necessary.

As we saw in Bornat *et al.*'s study, the 'biographical work' carried out by older people interviewed for research into the impact of family change appeared to enable them to construct a narrative coherence to their lives. Through this they were able to maintain their sense of identity in the face of personal disruption in the context of a public discourse of failure. This process of using life stories to maintain coherence within personal identities is explicit in work with children who have undergone frequent changes of care-giver in foster homes or residential units, with people with profound learning difficulties who are facing or who have experienced a significant transition in their living circumstances, and with older people in institutional care and with dementia.

For example, Middleton and Hewitt (2000) describe life-story work with people with profound learning difficulties who were moving from hospital to community-based care. This work was prompted in part by a recognition that nursing care plans, in spite of a terminology which suggests both a trajectory and a purpose to the provision of support, quite specifically failed to ensure any sense of continuity, history or future. Not only were such plans purely functionally based: concerned with issues such as eating and drinking, sleeping, and personal hygiene, they were also oriented solely to present circumstances – there could be no sense of change within these functional categories because old action plans were removed from case notes. Anyone coming new to a care team would not be able to tell whether the current functioning of any individual was better or worse than it had previously been. The functional nature of such 'plans' also meant that it would be possible for any two individuals to have identical plans – there was no sense of individual identity, the plans gave no indication that they related to a specific person with a past and future as well as a present, nor that the person had a life as well as a set of physiological functions which may change from time to time.

The life stories that were generated, in contrast, emphasised very individual aspects of people's histories and identities and recognised the significance of activities and behaviour that would be considered irrelevant in the context of a functional care plan. Such histories provided a means by which family members, staff and the person with learning difficulties could engage in a social practice of remembering – not only in the process of generating the narratives, but also once narratives had been created in the context of on-going conversations. Such stories were also a means by which it was possible to emphasise the agency of people whose care plans focused on how they needed to be looked after. The authors cite the example of a father describing incidents which made it clear that his profoundly disabled son not only was capable of expressing his pleasure at being able to make sounds with his wheelchair, but also remembered this experience so that he was able to recreate it ten years later when he was given a similar chair.

Communication with people with dementia can be difficult if the expectation is that their stories about their past, and present, are always accounts of real events. Instead they often need to be understood as constructions which express both emotional truthfulness and significant aspects of the person's identity. Crisp (1999) gives the example of her mother's claim to have designed the garden of the hospital in which she was currently living. This was evidently not the case, but could be understood as an indication of the importance to her mother both of recalling and communicating to others a specific activity, garden design, that had been something that she had undertaken on many occasions during her life, and also of expressing a continuing capacity to be creative: 'All those fragments of my mother's past gardening experiences, for example, had been woven into a coherent narrative about something that she had done – and in this very garden.' (p. 117) The sense of such a claim will be enhanced if the hearer is familiar with the history of the person concerned, but understanding the value of life stories as constructions in which people make meaning of their lives, rather than as reports of what happened at a specific point in time, is an important aspect of relating to people with dementia as people still able to construct their sense of self in relation both to themselves and others, rather than as people who have lost their personhood. Kitwood and Bredin (1992) argue the significance of the Other (a person or persons with whom they have a relationship of interdependence/dependence) for people with dementia to maintain their personhood: 'The Other is needed, not to work with growth, but to off-set degeneration and fragmentation...In terms of the metaphor of states of personhood, the self that is shattered in dementia will not naturally coalesce; the Other is needed to hold the fragments together' (p. 285). Story telling is one way of holding together the fragments.

Healing

I have referred to the use of life stories as one means of resisting the tendency for care to be reduced to responding to functional needs in the present. Mattingly (1998) develops this theme in her ethnography of the practice of occupational therapy with people who have experienced severe and life threatening injuries. She notes the power of narrative and the way in which people turn to this to make sense of extreme experiences which can fundamentally challenge not only their sense of self, but also threaten their survival. But she confirms the tendency identified by Middleton and Hewitt for professional practice to separate out one moment in a life – the injury and its aftermath, and within that moment to break down the elements of the 'problem' as currently experienced and to deal with each of these separately.

Mattingly's focus is primarily on the use of narrative within clinical encounters in which occupational therapists 'find themselves constantly confronted with the interpretative task of translating between their way of seeing and the patient's' (p. 74). She observed the effort that many occupational therapists (OTs) put into talking with patients and encouraging them to take part not only in a conversation about the therapy in which they were engaged, but also to become actual partners in the process. This urge to communicate extends even to patients who may be comatose and where the therapist is working on their body with no apparent sign that the person is aware of what they are doing. By trying to involve patients in a social process of constructing a story about the therapeutic process in which they are engaged, the therapist is emphasising both the personhood and the agency of the patient. They are working with hope that the person will be successful in the process of reconstructing their bodies and thus work to create success stories which reinforce evidence of progress. Such a process takes place in the present but with an awareness of a future and of a past in which the person was physically less able than they are now – after their accident and before they had started to engage in therapy. Mattingly understands the therapeutic process as a healing drama in which both the occupational therapist and the recipient are players.

Beyond the narrative of the therapeutic process itself, the patient is involved in an episode which is situated within their life story and which is likely to have a transformatory impact on future trajectories:

> The narrative meaning of any particular therapeutic episode must be embedded not only within the unfolding therapeutic narrative but also within a much broader narrative structure of a patient's life to which the therapist has not been privy. Even family narratives are sometimes imagined by therapists, who try to understand a family's past history and envision how that family history will change when the patient returns home. (pp. 98–9)

She illustrates this with the example of a therapist asked to work with a group of patients who had all experienced severe head injuries and who had been living in a long-stay residential facility from where few were discharged. The group was considered to be a disaster – many had stopped turning up and there was a sense that it was going nowhere. The OT brought in to work with these people tried to understand why it was not working and realised that it lacked a theme. As she reflected on this she thought about what she knew about the members of the group and realised that they were all young, wanted to get home and were from New York. From this emerged the notion that a theme for the group would be the New York subway. Activities based round this – writing graffiti, making giant pretzels and hot dogs, a trip to a simulated Central Park and filling an album with photos and newspaper cuttings – fulfilled a dual purpose of engaging the group in the type of exercises which would help the reconstruction of their physical capacities, and reconnecting them with their biographies through a journey which eventually took three members of the group back home.

Self-help, advocacy and campaigning

In each of the examples reviewed above, the process of generating stories about people's lives involved an interaction between a 'professional' of some description and the person whose story is being told. That professional could be a researcher, a residential care worker, a nurse, a counsellor, an occupational therapist or another worker in the field of health and social care. In each of these contexts there is a genuine wish for the story that is generated to express what is important for the person concerned, for it to reflect their personhood and agency and for it to contribute to a process of improving their personal situation and/or a more general understanding that can lead to improvements for others in similar situations. But narratives and life stories are also proving valuable for more political purposes in the context of autonomous action on the part of service users. There are a number of ways in which this is evident.

Stories told by people with mental health problems about their experiences, about what they have learned about how to survive such difficulties and what works and what doesn't work for them in terms of the type of services they receive have been vital in articulating an alternative version to the dominant medical perspective on mental illness, its causes and treatments. Such stories have been told by people who have become well known in the mental health user movement or who were already well known for other reasons: Judi Chamberlin's (1988) story recounted in *On Our Own* had a significant impact in the early days of the strengthening user/survivor movement in the late twentieth century, whilst Kate Millett (1991) brought her novelist skills to the telling of her story of living with what was diagnosed as manic depression in *The Loony Bin Trip*. Stories have been collected and published in order to try to increase others' understanding of the experience of mental health problems, to reduce the stigma attached to this and to explain how the experience of what some accept as madness is an integral part of people's lives (for example, Barker *et al.*, 1999; Leibrich, 1999). But others whose names will never be public have contributed their stories in forums where service users have come together or through research designed and carried out by users and survivors. For example, Barnes *et al.* (forthcoming) describe how women took the opportunity provided by work commissioned by the Department of Health in England on women-only mental health services to get on a soap box, or talk to a video camera about their lives and what they had learnt about what was important for women who come into contact with the mental health system. When those women told their stories they did not speak only about themselves as users of services, but as daughters, mothers, wives, friends and workers and they related their experiences of mental distress to other things that were happening in their lives and which needed to be understood to make sense of their distress.

Understanding the value of story telling in the development of the mental health user/survivor movement, or in the disability movement can be compared with the role played by the recounting of personal lives within the women's movement. Through making visible different personal histories, the way in which these are shaped by structural and cultural factors becomes evident, the relationship between the personal and the political can be understood and this can form the basis not only for individual advocacy but also for the development of alternative understandings and explanations which offer a fundamental challenge to the way in which we think about mental illness, about disability, about ageing or about care-giving. Young (2000) has expanded the concept of 'deliberation', often used to refer to dialogue between citizens and officials about issues of public policy, to include space for narrative as well as argument. She identifies different contexts in which the value of story telling has been recognised as a means of accessing the 'truth' or justness of a particular position or cause. She refers to the use of narrative in legal discussions and court-room settings 'as a means of challenging the idea that law expresses an impartial and neutral standpoint above all particular perspectives', and to a political function demonstrated by resistance movement leaders in Central and South America who

> narrate their life stories as a means of exposing to the wider literate world the oppression of their people and the repression they suffer from their governments. Often such *testimonios* involve one person's story standing for that of the whole group to a wider, sometimes global, public, and making claims upon that public for the group. (p. 71).

But service users often face difficulties when they seek to use stories in the context of dialogue with officials about policies, services and practices which might be more responsive to their needs and circumstances (M. Barnes, 2004). The nature of such stories is too often not understood and they are dismissed as 'mere anecdotes', unrepresentative of the experiences of others and thus unable to claim legitimacy as evidence on which to base policy.

Summary

In order to summarise this review of the different fields within which narratives and life stories are used in the context of health and social care it is useful to highlight what are the key characteristics of a narrative approach to life stories. Firstly, they encompass both past and future and they are told from a present that will be subject to change.

How the past is interpreted will depend on the particular perspective from which it is being viewed, and descriptions of both past and present will reflect what may be hoped or feared for the future. Life stories enable us to understand unique individuals in the context of their lives as a whole and do not pretend to define them solely by reference to their circumstances at the time at which they become the focus of attention – either of the researcher or the worker intervening in their lives for some therapeutic or care-giving purpose.

Because life stories reflect whole lives, they locate the individual within distinct historical time periods, within particular spaces and places, and within cultural, social, political and economic circumstances. For example, they enable us to understand how the experiences of old age may relate to those pertaining when people were young, and thus how old age may be experienced differently by different generational cohorts. They demonstrate the options that are open to people depending on structural factors such as social class, gender and ethnicity, and how different sources of oppression and marginalisation may affect the way in which disabled people, users/survivors of mental health services and lesbians and gay men, are able to construct their own identities.

The generation of life stories is a process through which those recounting their stories are making sense of their lives and creating coherence and meaning out of events and experiences. It is an active process which does not simply involve reviewing and recounting but rather a process through which the narrator is engaged in fashioning his or her identity. It is also a social process – the context in which narratives are generated influences the way they are told and what is said and what left out. The relationship between researcher, care worker or therapist and the person telling his or her story is crucial to what is produced. This is not a neutral process as far as the story tellers are concerned. They agree to tell their stories because they have a purpose in so doing. They may wish to get over a particular message, to access specific support, to present themselves in a particular way, or to use this opportunity to explore aspects of their lives they may not previously have thought too much about.

In the following three chapters I tell the stories of carers who were parents, sons and daughters, wives and husbands. I have presented them as distinct stories which require the coherence of the complete narrative in order to be understood. I have allocated the stories to one of the three chapters on the basis of the nature of the caring relationship that I knew about when I went to ask carers to tell me their stories. But, as will become evident, as they told their stories some people indicated that they had been involved in more than one type of caring relationship in the course of their lives. It is always hard and often not helpful to seek to assign people to categories which assume a single or fixed identity. But there were two reasons why I decided to keep to my decision to structure my initial discussion of carers' stories around the primary family relationship which had led to me carrying out the interview. Firstly, one of my aims in this book is to understand the way in which the experience of care-giving and the nature of the caring relationships in which these carers were involved was located within and shaped by particular histories and biographies. An important aspect of that is the nature of the relationship (if any) between care-giver and care-receiver before what became defined as 'caring' started. Secondly, as I will argue in this book, caring is something that is interwoven through many people's lives – it is a profoundly 'ordinary' experience. Yet particular relationships become designated as caring relationships at a particular point in time: for a variety of reasons, but not least because lay care-giving has now become officially recognised within social policy and by service providers. One effect of this is that such relationships become extracted from their contexts and may be regarded as extraordinary, with carers and caring relationships being pathologised, sanctified or pitied. None of those responses may be of most help to carers or those they support.

In these three chapters I tell summarised stories, based on narrative interviews with family carers, which have been checked out and confirmed by the carers themselves. They did not necessarily tell me their stories in chronological order as presented here, but apart from ordering their stories in this temporal frame, in what follows I have tried not to undertake any analysis or interpretation of what they told me.

The accounts of carers' lives were generated by means of interviews in which I invited the people concerned to tell me about their lives before and after they became carers. Ten of the twelve were identified through a carers' organisation and some of them – Lise, Nell, Violet and Pauline – I had worked with previously when I was involved in establishing a carers' group for research purposes. I already knew something about their circumstances, but I had never previously interviewed them about their lives. Six others offered to talk to me after I had given a presentation about what I hoped to do in this book at an annual meeting of a carers' organisation. Two other men offered to speak to me at this stage, but withdraw later: one by not coming to an arranged meeting and one telephoned to say that he had discussed this with his wife, whom he cared for, and she had not been happy about him taking part. My contact with Daniel came at the suggestion of one of the other carers I spoke to, whilst my contact with Alan came about through my own work networks.

All of the interviews took a long time – an hour and a half was the minimum, and one interview was spread over two meetings. One interview was conducted in my office, one in my home and all the others in the carers' homes. In some cases it was not only the care-giver I had gone to visit who was involved in the interview. When I arrived at Rose's house she was on the phone and I spoke briefly to Arif, her husband. Their daughter Surya was lying on the couch and, whilst I waited for Rose, Arif very tenderly adjusted her feeding tube. He was totally absorbed in Surya as he did so, leaning over her and talking to her, almost singing to her as he gazed into her eyes. Surya remained with us throughout my conversation with Rose, sometimes watching us talk and evoking a response from Rose or myself. When I arrived at Barbara's house I was met by her son William who engaged me in conversation. Just before I had finished talking to Barbara he came into the room and asked if he could talk to me. I had a long conversation with him after I had finished the interview with Barbara. I then spoke with Barbara's husband John who had been a nurse and who spoke of the importance of professionals who really listened to parents, who were independent, not simply doing what the 'bureau-crats' tell them, and of having one key worker who collects all the necessary life history information so that this does not have to be repeated to every worker who gets involved.

Gina's mother Irena was also present during the interview and involved from time to time in the discussion. She does not speak much English, but Gina checked out some points with her and I was able to have a brief exchange with her. Nell invited me to visit her son James to talk with him after I had talked to her, but this did not prove possible. When my interview with Emily had finished she invited me to stay to lunch. She showed me papers she had collected about social and health services and about carers and offered to let me have any of these that were of interest. I visited her on another occasion to go through her papers and took with me those that were of most interest.

I note these points in part because they were the source of information in addition to that which derived from what might be considered the 'formal' part of the narrative interview, but also because they offer some insights into the context within which it is possible to find out about carers' lives and situations. I return to this issue in Chapter 9 when I focus directly on the practice implications of a narrative approach to understanding care-giving.

The recordings of the interviews were transcribed and I then constructed the chronological summaries of their stories which form the basis for the accounts in the following chapters. Names were changed (some were chosen by the interviewees themselves) and certain details were left out to prevent people being identified, but nothing else was added or changed. I sent these summaries to the carers and asked them to check that I had got things right and to say if there was anything they wanted taken out of their stories before I used them in this book. Some clarifications and corrections were made at this stage, but nobody asked me to take anything out. Two carers said they had shown the summaries to close relatives or friends to ask for their views on what was written. One person added a quite substantial commentary to my summary and another wanted to expand and revise some of the ways in which I had expressed what had happened. For the purposes of this book I have had to make further edits in order to reduce the word length, but I have tried to leave most of these last two sets of amendments so that the stories appear as the carers themselves wanted.

CHAPTER 3

'Just a Mother'? Parenthood and Care- Giving with Disabled Children

In this chapter I tell the stories of five mothers of disabled children: Rose, Barbara, Pauline, Violet and Nell. Rose and Barbara's children were still young, while the other three women were supporting disabled sons and a daughter who were adults. Their stories reflect experiences of becoming a parent of a disabled child at different historical moments, as well as the different lengths of time for which they had been caring, although the birth of their child was not necessarily their first experience of care-giving. At the end of each story I provide a brief summary of key conceptual issues arising from these narratives, which I will develop in later chapters, and at the end of the chapter I reflect on the relationship between people's identities as carers and their personal biographies.

ROSE'S STORY
Rose and her husband Arif cared for their daughter Surya who was seven. Surya had a diagnosis of cerebral palsy and was severely physically and mentally impaired. They had a son, Magid, who was two years older than Surya.

Rose described her childhood and youth as one of six children in a Pakistani family in England. She left school when she was 14 because her father, who she described as 'strict and uneducated', thought she was hanging round with boys. She stayed at home and helped her mother in the house until she was 19 when she went to Pakistan to marry her third cousin. Five years later Arif was allowed to come to England. During that time she visited him in Pakistan and after three years of marriage she became pregnant. Her son Magid was born in England. Arif finally got a visa when Magid was four months old, came to England and found a job in a factory. Surya was born 13 months later. Rose and her new family lived with her mother for 18 months.

Rose described the point at which they realised something was wrong with Surya. At four months she started vomiting and having diarrhoea and was admitted to hospital. Rose stayed with her as she was breast-feeding and said she was scared that something was seriously wrong with her daughter. Surya couldn't roll or hold anything. Doctors told Rose they thought Surya's development was delayed. When she asked them questions, their response was to say 'Don't worry, she is slow.' When I asked Rose how she thought the doctors treated her at this time she said: 'It seems like they had children all the time and seems like, it's nothing for them, you know. The way they were treating me. Now I am saying looking back, I am saying that the way they were treating me like, they all treat me good and everything, checking and everything. They all think nothing of it.'

Rose described how the health visitor saw her put Surya in a baby walker. The health visitor told her she should not do this as it was not good for her, but it wasn't until Surya was 11 months old that a doctor at the Child Development Centre told Rose that Surya's brain was damaged. Even then the doctor didn't use the words 'cerebral palsy' – it was the health visitor who eventually told her the diagnosis and that it was serious.

Rose described her response when she was finally told what was wrong with Surya: 'I was really like in shock...I didn't know cerebral palsy, 'cause another kid, the mother was there as well and he had cerebral palsy and his head was like really down, he was severe like. At that time you know my daughter was as well, but her head was not really floppy...But I was really crying and you know making me [pause] calm me down and everything. So (pause) I was sort of like in shock. Slowly, slowly they were telling me all these things...They did all these tests, nerves and [pause] MRI [magnetic resonance imaging] scan and all these tests. And then they told me cerebral palsy like...Yes, big shock.'

Rose said that she eventually calmed down, because she realised it was not an illness like cancer and that her daughter would live, even if she did not have a long life. It was clear that Rose and Arif loved Surya very much:

ROSE: It's like, you know, when we take her, you know when we get out the house or something, it's like something missing [laughter]. We get like, we get mad or something.

MB: What, because she's not there?

ROSE: Yes…It's like we're used to her now…

MB: You like being with her?

ROSE: Yes, it's hard…Even though she has all this disability, just finding you know [pause] as long as she's um, you know alive like, we will cope.

At seven Surya had poor eyesight and wore glasses. She couldn't sit up on her own or walk. Special exercise equipment designed to strengthen her legs had been recommended by a physiotherapist and provided as a result of a charity raising £2000. Rose and Arif demonstrated this to me whilst we spoke. Rose said Surya enjoyed using it and this certainly appeared to be the case. Rose said they were meant to use it everyday, but they tended to forget.

As Surya was using the equipment, Rose spoke about her capacity to understand when people were talking about her, the fact that her hearing was good and how she often laughed when people talked to her. She also reacted to emotions – if anyone argued or fought she got scared. Rose reflected on the fact that Surya's reactions to emotions and her capacity to feel were well developed even though she could not speak. Rose then spoke about her distress that her parents did not appreciate what Surya was capable of:

> You know like my parents are very uneducated and they are very negative people and everything…They don't live with her twenty-four hours a day. We know how she feels and we know what she understands and everything. If she was there, my son was just that way and he was playing and she was – her eyes would go towards him. And she was looking at him and my dad couldn't believe it. He said that she knows her brother. The way she was looking at him was like, she was looking at him upside down…her head was there and she was looking there and her eyes were on him…she is very clever in that sense, that she knows…

Rose also described how Surya moved her lips in response when they spoke directly to her as if she was trying to reply to them. She summed this up by saying: 'even though you know she got cerebral palsy we think that, you know she – even though she is disabled she has got some things she understands.'

I asked Rose what a typical day was like. 'I tell you in the morning about what we do. Like, give her the feed [she is fed through a tube] and then we bring her, carry her down. And we put her here and the carer comes in. We have a carer for one hour. She washes her and cleans her, brushes her teeth and everything, wash and everything like that. And does a massage, the exercise. Because you know when she wakes up, she's stiff.'

Rose went on to say that even if Surya was on the settee or on the floor they had to be aware of her all the time in case she fell, or removed the feeding tube, or her glasses slipped down her face. She attended a special school that Rose said she enjoyed, but often made her tired. In the afternoon a carer came for two hours to give her a bath or wash and to massage her again. She received this help seven days a week.

Rose talked about the way in which she had learnt about Surya's responses to what was going on around her, and was able to anticipate when she was likely to have a fit. She compared this to the way in which parents of a 'normal child' learn to read the signals and knew what their children were trying to do. She illustrated how paid workers wanted to access that knowledge: during the summer holidays Surya went on a play scheme and Rose was asked to write down what she did and did not like doing. She told the workers that Surya liked noisy things and attention, being with other children, but did not like fighting, scary noises or shouting.

I asked how other children in the neighbourhood responded to Surya. Rose said they used to tease Magid that he had a handicapped sister and looked suspiciously at her when Rose took her out to sit on the front step. But this now happened less often. She used to get angry but she had got used to it. She also talked about the 'look' that people gave Surya when she took her out on the bus, but also said bus drivers helped her with the buggy.

I asked Rose whether she ever felt angry about having a disabled child. Her reply was: 'Um yes I did, I feel angry – I think why is it me, why shouldn't it be my sister, or why couldn't it be my brother's children? [Laughter] That's how I feel I guess.'

She told me her sisters said that she should pray more often and good things would happen. She was obviously annoyed about this, saying that she might not pray five times a day, but she did pray. She then went on to talk about the very limited help she got from her family: 'because they know she has epilepsy and they say that they get scared'. Her older sister had started to phone sometimes, but she only visited every six months. Her mother only came if it was urgent, although she visited Rose's other sister every two weeks.

Rose talked about how tiring it was looking after Surya. She was also obviously worried about her daughter's health. She described how Surya was twice admitted to the Intensive Treatment Unit as a result of chest infections and she was scared on those occasions – the doctors had asked her what she wanted them to do if Surya were to become really ill: 'I said to them I don't want nothing happening to her. Yes, even now they say to me that, um, what if she goes really ill and what do you want her to be alive or what? And I just say, no I want her to be alive, I don't want her to die.'

I asked Rose if there was anyone who came to support *her*. She said: 'Yes, I do have someone, …But it's not quite a lot really, it's not often, couple of months. She does come but it's like, she fills in forms and something like that. But I don't sometimes get the time to talk, not that much. When I feel really emotional like, then I do cry or whatever…you know, like counselling, I don't talk that much…it's only when I am really upset'. Rose said she found it particularly hard when Surya had a fit because she had been told she could die in a fit.

Towards the end of the interview I asked Rose if she had thought about any ways in which she might want to use what she had learnt from caring for Surya. She said she had started to attend college to improve her maths and English because she had left school so early. She had also discovered that she had dyslexia. She was learning to drive so she could take her daughter out. Arif had decided he wanted to be a teacher and he was about to start college.

Rose also spoke about her involvement with carers' groups. She said she found it helpful to find things out and share ideas with other carers. She also spoke of the way paid carers who came from social services learnt from her. She described one of the carers who visited as being quite rich so she did not have to work, but said that she did so because she learnt so much from the children she worked with, not only about them but about life. Rose and she talked a lot during her visits and learnt from each other.

Rose and Arif had saved to buy a bigger house that they could have adapted so they no longer had to carry Surya upstairs. When I interviewed Rose they had been waiting a long time for the adaptations to be done and had been told this would take between six months and a year. They had decided that they would need to move before the work was completed, otherwise they would have to pay council tax on two houses.

Rose said she hoped that Surya could learn to crawl so she could move on her own, but apart from this she didn't know what to hope for in terms of her future. She said it was up to God what would happen; she didn't want to plan for the future, she just wanted to take every day as it came.

Rose's story raises a number of issues which I will develop in later chapters when I offer conceptual analyses of care and care-giving:

- It highlights the significance of the particularity of the knowledge that care-givers develop and the way in which this contributes to the way they think about issues of rights: of those they care for and themselves.
- It demonstrates the importance of 'attentiveness' to the needs of others and of paying attention to the position of the care-receiver from their perspective.
- It suggests that the availability of a service (such as adaptations to a house to make life easier for disabled people and those who care for them) cannot be considered to be delivered 'competently' unless it is also delivered in a timely manner.
- And it illustrates that care needs to be addressed to one's self as well as others (for example, Rose's decision to pick up her education again).

BARBARA'S STORY

Barbara had cerebral palsy and had cared for her mother when she developed cancer and her father James when he developed a degenerative condition. She and her husband John were caring for their son William who had been diagnosed as autistic.

Barbara was one of six children. She went to an ordinary school – she could walk but dragged one of her legs and got very tired so her mother had to collect her in a pushchair. She said that when she was learning anything new she would dribble and described how her mother hid a bib inside her clothing so it didn't point her out as being different. Her mother also used a mouth organ to build up her mouth muscles to help her talk.

Barbara started her story by identifying the first time she became a carer. When she was 12 she held and calmed a fellow pupil whom the teachers didn't know how to handle: 'And that's when it all started. They started pushing me into child care, etc., caring for people. I cared for my mother who had cancer. I cared for my father'. Her father 's heart disease caused muscular wasting. Barbara used to deal with James's medication and lift and wash her mother when she became too weak to do so herself. Her mother died when Barbara was 21.

In her late teens Barbara worked in different caring jobs – she talked about being a houseparent in a children's residential home and working in another home looking after babies and toddlers. After her mother died she went into nursing for 13 years, mainly in mental health care.

Barbara had a close relationship with her father. When I asked her what she felt about looking after him she paused and said it was 'just part of general life'. James lived with Barbara during his illness and she described going out to work as a nurse then coming home and nursing her father. They had assistance with the housework from local authority social services and when Barbara came home from work she would sit with James and talk to him to 'keep him in touch'. She said sometimes he would get cross and feel that what was happening to him was unfair. Barbara said her sister suggested he should go into a nursing home but he didn't want to do that and cried when this was suggested. James was ill for 5–6 years before he died, in hospital, after having been admitted with a broken arm. He was 60 and Barbara was 28.

Barbara said she carried on working as a nurse after her father died. She went to Malta and Egypt for holidays. Her father had left her a bit of money and she had her own house so she thought she was 'well looked after'.

Five years later she married and moved to another part of the country. Her first pregnancy ended in a miscarriage. Barbara conceived again, nearly miscarried again, but as a result of treatment throughout her pregnancy she carried to term and William was born. Barbara described her experience of childbirth. A few days before the birth it was discovered that part of her lower spine was missing which meant she had to have a caesarean section: 'I was in a wheelchair for nearly ten days after the birth…It was a difficult birth, in the end. Um, they let me treat him as a normal baby, but I was in a wheelchair, that's the only difference'.

Her husband John was with her much of this time, helping her deal with the considerable pain she was in. She told me that at one point John brought the baby to her and she told him to take him away as she didn't want to have anything to do with him. Barbara said that, immediately after he was born, a doctor noted that William had a problem with his back, but this appeared to right itself quickly. But her experience as a disabled child and her awareness of her own need to look after herself led her to decide: 'When he started clinging to me I said, oh no, I am not having this. I can't. So we got him – through Social Services – a childminder. Previously to that I wasn't sleeping, I wasn't eating, I was depressed. I had depression, severe depression after William was born.'

Barbara said William had no speech until he started school. He also continued to wet the bed beyond the age when most children would be dry. She had to wake him up during the night to take him to the toilet to get over this. Barbara said she thought she might end up in a wheelchair so she encouraged William to do things for himself – like asking for things in cafés when they went out:

> It was safety for him and it was safety for me as well. I wasn't not trying to get attached to him, but I was trying to be practical with it as well. Um, [pause] one of my husband's friends at his work had William off us for a couple of nights, or for one night for me. Just before I went in for a review meeting, as a baby. Um, beforehand I was literally doped up to the eyeballs, no painkillers, nothing, but I was just very very drained. The next time the woman saw me, she said something has happened. You look more aware, more bright, more able to cope. I said someone has had him for me for the night. [Laughter]

Barbara used this experience to make a plea for social workers to understand how valuable this sort of back-up system can be for parents who become exhausted looking after disabled children.

William attended a mainstream school with a specialist speech and language unit attached. He received intensive input on his speech, which Barbara said he really enjoyed. He had been diagnosed as autistic. At nine William left the specialist unit and went into the mainstream school where he had the support of a classroom assistant. When I spoke to her Barbara was concerned about suggestions that his educational statement (identifying him as having special educational needs) would be removed when he moved into secondary school. She described the move to secondary school as 'the next nightmare'. She was worried that there would be more chance of him getting hurt in secondary school and thought it important that he retained his statement in order to ensure the funding was available to provide him with additional support. She felt she was engaged in a bit of a battle over this, although was glad he would be going to a mainstream school.

Barbara described William as 'having a way with him': he was not embarrassed about engaging with adults and 'can click with anybody'. But she worried that he was too trusting and said she watched him all the time so that she always knew where he was and what he was doing. Sometimes he called out to people he didn't know in public places, but usually people treated him very well. Although William told me people sometimes made fun of him because of his weight and he didn't like bullies.

Once a month William went to a residential unit for disabled children to give Barbara and John 24 hours for themselves. I asked Barbara what he felt about this: 'If he goes in with the right people, yes, with his own ability. When it comes to the docile ones, forget it, he hates it.' When I spoke to William after talking to his mother he reinforced this. He also talked about how much he liked living with his parents and how he'd like to see his grandmother more often, but she lived five hours away.

I asked Barbara if they were planning beyond secondary school, but Barbara said they wanted to get over the move to secondary school first. She described good days and bad days – on the bad days she wanted William to stay out of her way. She said she had felt hard done by, but now 'You are here to live and that's the end of it.' She was involved in a number of groups: based around the school and carers' groups. She said these got her out of the house and stopped her vegetating. She was also going to college once a week.

Key issues

- The identities of 'care giver' and 'care receiver' do not necessarily describe different people: disabled people can be carers.
- Personal and professional can come together in understanding people's identities as carers.
- Care-giving can often be seen as a 'taken for granted' aspect of everyday life.
- Caring for oneself is as important as caring for others.

PAULINE'S STORY

Pauline and Bill adopted Simon when he was five, knowing he was 'quite mentally handicapped'. As an adult it was also suspected that he had mental health problems. After a number of difficult incidents Simon had been admitted to a secure residential unit where he was at the time of the interview. He was 29. Pauline was living on her own after Bill's death.

Pauline described her childhood as an only child. Her disabled grandmother lived with them until she was admitted to hospital, then to a long stay unit. Pauline trained as a nurse and worked in an acute hospital. She also worked in a children's hospital where she had some experience of working with disabled children.

Pauline married Bill when she was in her late 20s. She said they were both financially quite secure and decided to start a family, but she discovered she could not conceive. They adopted a baby daughter, Jackie, she gave up paid work and they became foster parents.

Pauline spoke about their difficulties in adopting another child. Because there were fewer babies available for adoption they explored the possibility of adopting a disabled child. She said they felt they had a lot to offer, including financial security, and 'We felt that whoever we fostered we would be on shifting sand all the time, and we felt the child deserved the security of family life...And we felt we deserved the security of being able to put our all into bringing up a child'.

However, they discovered they had been crossed off the foster parent list by the local authority and said this appeared to mean they were unsuccessful in their applications to adoption societies. They appealed to the Ombudsman. Pauline described the way in which this experience put her and Bill into a 'fighting mood' and said: 'I think [laughter] looking back it stood us very well indeed because we realised that we were going to be – had to be in fighting mood for many, many things.'

Pauline said they responded to an advert placed by a local authority in another part of the country and adopted a five-year-old boy. Pauline described Simon when he first came to live with them:

> I felt that I could never take my eyes off him, because of course he was disorientated. He had come from many, many miles away, where the customs, the dialect and way of life was very, very different. He moved around a great deal. He was very under nourished.

Simon could understand what was said to him but he was unable to reply. Pauline said that when he wanted something to eat he would point and say 'mmmm'. If he wanted attention he would grab hold of a sleeve and hang on. He couldn't dress himself and he was clumsy, although he could feed himself and use the toilet. Pauline described her GP's response when she took Simon to be registered with him. He said 'Why did you adopt that?' and added that he would never speak. Pauline said her response to this was 'I thought, right, Mister. We will see about that...I thought, well, I can never let go of this child.'

Pauline described the difficulties they faced trying to find a school for Simon: 'There was a big barny before he started school, because he was five and a half when he came to us and nobody seemed to be getting their finger out about what school he should start at.' Pauline said she was worried about the delay because he needed speech therapy. No playschool would accept him because he was beyond school age and she said she was getting weary looking after him all day. Pauline described taking Simon to her local councillor's house and demanding to see him and telling him he had to find a school place for Simon who was now nearly six. She said Simon 'did his high pitched screaming act' in front of the councillor and soon after this she received a letter asking her to go for an interview with the head of a special school.

Pauline expressed dissatisfaction with the school Simon attended: 'Simon settled down, but I didn't think much of it, to be frank. It seemed to me in a lot of cases just like a glorified playgroup.' He only received speech therapy for half an hour a week and Pauline said no one apart from his family could understand him.

Pauline spoke about the financial impact of having two children. Simon needed special clothing and things in the house were getting damaged. She described how she had to fight to receive child benefit. She decided to use the benefit to pay for a private speech therapist who came to the house every week for two to three years until Simon learnt to speak.

Pauline said Jackie got jealous of this so she got her involved in the process of helping him with his exercises. Simon learnt to ride a tricycle, but bullies used to come after him and batter his bike. Pauline said the first words he learnt to speak were four-letter words, but life got easier once he could speak because people weren't so frightened and were more willing to acknowledge him: 'And actually, gradually, and it was like the seven wonders of the world, it really was.'

Throughout her narrative Pauline spoke of her dissatisfactions with social workers. She said they seemed to have little knowledge of 'mental handicap' and no one told her about support groups that were available. But once she and Bill had adopted Simon their anxiety that he might be removed went away and they had no further contact with social services for many years.

Pauline described fitting her life around Simon. He was picked up by coach at 8 a.m. to get to school and had to be met at 3 p.m. Pauline got a job in a clinic but she described as 'nerve racking' ensuring that the timing worked out. 'And then all of a sudden they say we are going to put him in a taxi. And I thought, yippee, no standing on that freezing cold corner. Well that was worse because the taxi, you never knew what time it would come, and sometimes he would come at 8.30, even 9.40. Well I couldn't leave the house until he had gone. And of course I would be even later for the clinic then, and they were getting very fed up with it.' She joined an employment agency for greater flexibility. But as well as being really hard work bringing up Simon it was also extremely interesting to see the way in which he developed. He put on weight and starting to develop confidence. Pauline described him as 'like a little squirrel'. Things would go missing and they would discover he had hidden them away.

Pauline recounted a number of incidents that demonstrated the demands of caring for Simon. She spoke of wishing for a period of respite when she and Bill could 'just flop'. However when Simon went away with a family for a weekend he fell down a hill and broke an arm and was in plaster for two months. Pauline said that far from enabling her and Bill to have some rest they ended up having to go back and forwards to have his arm re-plastered.

She also talked of sources of support. They found out about a church that had a monthly group for disabled children. She said: 'it felt as though we were part of a community'. They found out about Mencap [a voluntary organisation] 'by accident' but most of the members had known each other for a long time and she and Bill did not really feel they fitted in because most had adult sons and daughters.

When Simon was 10 Bill developed a chronic disabling disease and had to give up work. Pauline said: 'As my husband suddenly became ill, so Simon – as the one was starting to go down, the other one was coming up.' Pauline gave up work to look after Bill as well as her children. Simon was about to move into secondary school and Pauline spoke of her determination to find a school she thought would be right for him:

> I did a lot of scouting around...I used to look to see what the kids were like, you know, to sense the atmosphere, were the teachers looking bored, did they look purposeful. You know you get the ambience ...I put in that I wanted him to go to XXXXX and they fought me tooth and nail over it. And all of a sudden they capitulated.

I asked Pauline how other people treated Simon. She said that at school he was not bothered about being different from other children, but neighbourhood children used to mock him. He went out on his bike, played with other children in the fields and learnt to fight his own battles. He learnt to dress himself slowly and tie his shoelaces. He got a lot of head colds and his breath started to smell, which caused other children to make fun of him. But a minor operation improved his tendency to get colds and his eczema, which Pauline said was a good indication of his equilibrium, also started to get better. She described how as he grew into adolescence he became quite good-looking and took more care over his appearance.

I asked Pauline how her relationship with Simon changed as he grew older and she gave the following example:

> I used to get the Peter and Jane books, I don't know whether you remember them – most boring books on God's earth, you know. And I used to sit him down beside me for about fifteen minutes and try to push him through stage 1. You know, Peter and Jane go in the garden, you know, I mean soul destroying, you know [laughter]. I mean I could

do that to a degree, and then suddenly he didn't want Mother telling him how to add up or read, it wasn't done, you know.

The next transition in Simon's life – leaving school – was also described by Pauline as a time of tension. First she spoke about their reasons for wanting Simon to go to a residential college:

> we thought when he was in his twenties he should definitely go away somewhere to a college or wherever, and learn to look after himself. You know, because I thought well, he better because we won't—I was suddenly aware that my husband was ill and I was aware of our own mortality.

She learnt that if they waited until he was 20 for him to go to a residential college they would have to pay, but if he were to go when he was 16, the local education authority (LEA) would pay for the three years from 16 to 18. But the authority resisted paying for Simon to go to a college outside the area. Eventually Pauline said that if they could find somewhere within the area where he could learn independent living skills they would agree to Simon going there. Nowhere suitable was found and eventually the LEA agreed to fund a place elsewhere.

Pauline described the day they took Simon to the residential college as a bitterly cold day when she felt numb from the cold but also numb that they were leaving him. She said it was a hard but important transition for both of them. Simon was at the college for three years and then spent a year in linked semi-independent accommodation. After four years at the college Simon came back to his parents' house. Pauline's story of this stage of their lives recounted a number of points of tension. Simon started off on a work placement but when this finished he spent most of his day watching television. Pauline said he could cook 'to a degree', but she did all his washing and tidied up after him. He had a number of girlfriends and Pauline was concerned that he might father a child. Bill's illness was becoming worse and he spent longer spells in hospital. Problems developed between Simon and Bill:

> my husband was getting quite jealous of him I think…He [Simon] was this virile quite good-looking young fella, whereas he, because of his illness was losing his looks you know…They were always having a go at one another. Well, I mean this time I was starting to work shifts and sometimes nights. And I'd come home and sometimes off a late shift, and they both met me in the hall and Simon would be saying 'Dad wouldn't let me have the football on, blah blah blah', and my husband would say, 'What do you think, I just turned over the football for the news or I just such and such'.

During this period Pauline's 88-year-old mother collapsed and was rushed into hospital. She was discharged into a nursing home. Pauline said this was a hard thing to do but she did not think she had any choice as she could not have cared for Simon, Bill and her mother under one roof.

Pauline said that when Bill died it was a big shock for Simon and he became 'a bit of a handful' after this. He had occasional short-term placements but most of the time he was at home. He had a girlfriend and Pauline said she discovered her family were getting money off him. Things reached crisis point when Pauline and Simon had a row and Simon threatened her physically. The next day Pauline sought help from a social worker who offered no help so she went to the police. She said they advised her to go to her solicitor to get an affidavit setting out all she had told the police about Simon's behaviour and the lack of help she had received and to send this to all those agencies with which he had contact, but she received no response to this.

Eventually a male social worker found a residential unit for Simon. But as Pauline's story demonstrated, this was not the end of the challenges she faced in looking after him. After he had been in the unit for about a year she received a phone call from the police as a result of an incident involving Simon and his girlfriend. The result of this was that he was admitted to a secure unit in a learning disabilities hospital. He stayed there for three months and then was admitted to a specialist unit further away. He was in this unit at the time that I spoke to Pauline.

Whilst he was in the unit he developed a relationship with another girl and the two of them ran off together. Pauline was really worried, but then found he had broken into her house and taken money from it. She started legal proceedings but was told she would not succeed because of his mental state. She said she was furious with him. She said Simon liked to manipulate people but could also 'charm the socks off people' when he wanted.

I asked her what she thought about what had happened to Simon, and whether she felt he had received appropriate help:

I really don't know what to think about any of it [pause]. I mean [pause] you know, I mean he is an adult; he is responsible for his actions. You can only advise him...He had a lot of privileges when he was there on informal. They were working for him to go back into the community. You know he could come out and about with me at the weekend, he might go to such and such a place, you know, and he blew it.

When I asked Pauline to reflect back she said she had never regretted adopting Simon. She said people's mouths dropped open and they changed the subject when she talked about her experiences of looking after him. In contrast, she had become friends with a woman she met through Mencap who had a disabled son who lived in a residential unit and who sometimes used to visit Simon with her. Pauline said they could have a good laugh because they both understood what it was like. She had started going to meetings of Rethink (formerly National Schizophrenia Fellowship) and described this as being 'like coming home from a foreign country – suddenly everyone understands'.

Pauline's story has not got an ending, but she spoke of how, because Simon was in a residential unit, she could please herself about when and what she ate, lead her own life and do the things that pleased her. She was still involved with carers' groups – she had been going for over 20 years, but was thinking that there were other more enjoyable things that she would like to do and she didn't tell people that she was a carer. She said her relationship with Simon had altered her personality and made her a much stronger person. But she also thought that 'Sadly, I find I haven't got much sympathy with cosseted and help-less women.'

Post script: When I spoke to Pauline some months later she said Simon had recently moved into a small residential unit where he appeared to be getting on well with other residents and looking after himself better. She was feeling more positive about his future.

Key issues

- Pauline's narrative expressed a strong sense that it was necessary to fight for justice for both Simon and herself, and that it was down to her to do this. Her account suggests that her rights and his rights were interwoven.
- Her account also demonstrates that care-giving involves suspending one's own plans and goals in order to be attentive to the needs of others.
- She suggests that those who receive care are not absolved of the responsibility of being attentive to care-givers.
- Her story also suggests the significance of shared experience as a basis for both personal support and effective advocacy.

VIOLET'S STORY

Violet was born in Jamaica into a large family. She and her husband Samuel came to England to work. Her four children joined them later. Her daughter Gloria had an accident when she was six and gradually became more severely impaired. She was 43 and living with her parents when I spoke to Violet. Violet speaks with a strong Jamaican accent and it was not possible to obtain a transcript of my interview with her.

Violet described her childhood in rural Jamaica as one of nine children. Her father died when she was a baby and one of her siblings died in childhood, but she said her mother remained strong in the face of these deaths. She joined Samuel in England in 1962 and they had lived in the same area of the same city ever since.

She described how Gloria hit her head badly and as a result suffered brain damage. Violet said she was really upset by the accident because no one told her what was wrong with her daughter. She received lots of different messages, but no one gave Gloria any help. Violet contrasted this experience with someone else she knew who had received considerable help following an accident and who had recovered well as a result. Violet said that at first it was thought that Gloria was not affected too badly. She could still walk and run, she mixed a lot and got on well with her three brothers, but she had epileptic fits.

Violet described how Gloria's health started deteriorating during her teens. When Gloria was in her early 20s Violet left her in a respite care home whilst she visited relatives in Jamaica and when she returned was told Gloria had had a stroke. After this Gloria became severely disabled and could not walk or feed herself. Violet described how she had to provide considerable physical care for her, including turning her during the night, as she was unable to move herself.

Gloria had been attending a day centre every day apart from weekends and holidays for two years. Violet said that Gloria enjoyed this as staff took her out in a minibus and to buy clothes. She commented 'they're real carers'. She also noted that they tended to spoil Gloria: 'Everything she says she wants, they give her, then when she comes home and she doesn't get it she gets angry!' Violet described Gloria's response to her impairments and to those who looked after her. She said Gloria sometimes got angry with herself because she couldn't do things. For example, she loved books but was frustrated that she couldn't turn the pages. Violet said she could also be quite moody and: 'I just have to tell her to stop until she calms down.' In both the day centre and the respite home there were people with the right attitude, so Gloria had no problem being in those places. Violet said Gloria did not mind people coming to wash and dress her, and she did not think her daughter was embarrassed at receiving personal care as long as it was provided by people 'who are loving', but she did get upset when people looked at her. Violet said Gloria had stopped going to church because people used to ask her what was wrong with her. She could also get angry at the way she was treated by service providers. Violet described an occasion when Gloria was having physiotherapy and told her mother she was angry about what was being done to her. Violet said she wanted to be there whilst her daughter was receiving the treatment, but was not allowed.

Violet showed me the adaptations that had been made to the house. Gloria's bedroom was linked to her parents' room via a connecting door. Her bed was electronic and could be raised to enable her to sit partially upright to watch TV. It also had a massage function. The bathroom had a wide door and a shower with a chair. There was also a commode that Violet helped her to use. A lift enabled Gloria to get upstairs.

Violet said she had to be quite assertive to get these adaptations. Service providers had suggested that her daughter should go into a home and when Violet refused this they suggested that a bedroom and toilet should be created downstairs. But Violet insisted that Gloria should be able to stay upstairs so that she was near to her and Samuel during the night. The local authority social services department would not provide an electronic bed and eventually Violet bought this with financial help from her sons – it cost £1500. In recounting how she had had to negotiate about these adaptations Violet said 'I had to fight and phone and phone and phone and phone. I wouldn't give up.'

Gloria had been assessed by the Independent Living Fund for financial assistance, but when I spoke to Violet she said they had not received the money and she was very concerned about it. This had been intended to enable them to pay for someone not only to help Gloria when she was not at the day centre, but also to take her out. Violet said she could not push Gloria in her wheelchair, as she was too heavy. They were receiving help from a bathing and dressing service in the mornings and at night and had a care plan that included two-week periods of respite care. Violet was most positive about the help she received from a local carers' centre. She said they had given her a grant to go on holiday and if she needed any assistance she went to this centre rather than to her social worker because she found the staff and talking to other carers more helpful.

Violet told me that Gloria would like to move into her own place but she needed constant support. Violet was adamant that she wouldn't put her in a home. She said that although looking after her was hard, she was not a problem and reflected that in Jamaica it was taken for granted that everyone would look after everyone else. If there was a disabled child it made no difference, the whole family was involved. I asked Violet what Samuel thought and she replied that he had 'no choice' about having a disabled daughter. She told me that he and her grandson help out, and she also received help from a woman who lived nearby.

I observed a number of religious references in Violet's living room and I asked her about her faith. She said Christianity was important and helped her to cope. She went to church every Sunday but said she could not do as much with the church as she used to as she had to be there when Gloria came home. Violet said she sometimes got angry that she didn't receive the support she would like to help her look after Gloria, but she distinguished that from being angry that she had a disabled daughter and said she would not give up on her – 'if it were me I wouldn't let nobody give up on me, so why should I give up?' Violet described her approach as taking one thing at a time and trying not to worry. She said she put her trust in God and prayer helped her. She acknowledged that it was hard being a carer but harder if there was no one to help and that she did not feel alone. She reflected that those who make decisions about what support carers and disabled people get could find themselves in a similar situation, and also that if she was disabled she would not want to be in a home.

Key issues

- Violet's account emphasises the importance of understanding how disabled people respond to the care they receive.
- She emphasised the universality of care-giving and receiving: anyone could find themselves in this situation.
- Violet illustrated the way in which care-givers seek to 'stand up for the rights' of those they care for, but her account did not reflect a sense of unfairness in the situation she was in.
- Violet unquestioningly accepted her responsibility to care for her daughter and located this within the cultural context of her childhood.

'NELL GWYNN'S' STORY

Nell was caring for her adult son James who was living in his own flat, supported by care assistants, when I interviewed her. Nell's husband, Charles, had died when she was 46 and she was living with a new partner in what she described as an unsatisfactory relationship. She had an older son Derek who lived some distance away.

Nell's account of her life before James's birth was brief. She said she was the middle daughter of nine children and was brought up to think that girls should not expect to have a career, but should find a man to marry and have children. She had her first son, Derek, when she was 18 and James when she was 21.

Nell described James's early years and her experiences of the unsympathetic way she and he were treated. When he was three he was diagnosed with cystic fibrosis. By the time he was six he had started falling and it was obvious he wasn't developing properly. He was subjected to extensive tests that revealed he didn't have cystic fibrosis but did not come up with a clear diagnosis. Nell said that after one batch of tests the doctor told her that James would be dead in 12 months and she should 'take him home and love him'.

Nell described this as a turning point in her life: '...the rest of your family is just pushed to one side. You're all torn, you are all really torn and I wanted to pack as much life into James's short life as possible.'

She changed jobs, it had a significant effect on her relationship with her husband and she said she was often very resentful of James, although she worshipped him. She said she did things with James that mothers wouldn't usually do: 'I've been to Rock concerts with a leather jacket with a skull and crossbones on my back because I wanted James to experience Rock.' The family always went on holiday together – Nell said she and Charles never had a holiday on their own after James was born.

Nell expanded on the impact of having a disabled son. In the early days they received no help caring for James. They often drank at home because it was hard to go out. At New Year's Eve they hired a hall and put on a disco for themselves and other families. She said when James was young people didn't accept the inconvenience of wheelchairs coming in so they got 'shunted away and isolated'. Nell said it affected her relationships, including her sex life. Charles had a nervous breakdown because he thought James's disability was in some way his fault because he had been illegitimate. Nell spoke of how hard it was to have a 'normal' adolescent son, James, and a 'husband going nutty'. She recounted an incident when they were on holiday and Derek came running into the tent crying because other children were calling James a spastic. She said Derek wanted to fight the world for James. I asked her if she felt she was fighting and she replied: 'Fighting? I have always fought one system or another. And I feel I have achieved a lot from the fighting'.

She described as bereavement the emotions she had gone through when her hopes and expectations about her child were dashed:

> when you're pregnant you think your child will be prime minister or play for England, or whatever your aspirations are. And then you have to let go of all these things, like they are never going to get a job, and they are never going to have a family, they are never going to be able to give you grandchildren [pause] and they are never really going to be able to survive without people around them.

She said at times she was angry with James and with God, but she also questioned whether his disability was her fault. She thought she over-compensated for James's disability and that this was probably in part to blame for the fact that he became a very effective manipulator.

Nell described her relationship with her husband as one in which they fought like cats and dogs but could still be very passionate with each other. Very early in her narrative she told me that Charles had died of a heart attack when she was 46. He died in August and that September was the first time that they had arranged respite care for James so they could go on holiday together. At that stage of her life Nell said it was still important to her to have a man, but she said she wondered who else would want her with 'this baggage' [James]. She said she undervalued herself because she didn't know who would want her, but she wanted to replace what she had lost. The result of this was that she 'picked up some rubbish'. She got into a relationship with a man who had no home or job who, she thought, would be grateful for what she could offer and would not be resentful of James.

Nell described her husband's death as a tragedy for James as well as for her. This was compounded by James's girlfriend dying suddenly not long after. Then:

NELL: I had the audacity to have a heart attack. And I couldn't do an awful lot for James which I think he was quite…

MB: Quite cross with you about that, was he?

NELL: Yes, because like everybody around him had popped off and now 'My mother dearest to me'…You know there was a lot of anger there and a lot of resentment and, it's like before I had always just thrown his wheel-chair around…And then suddenly I couldn't do it for James.

James hit a woman at the day centre and Nell put this down to the anger he was feeling at this time. She said staff wanted to suspend him and Nell refused to support James by defending his action. This had significant consequences. Soon after, Nell had been at a party and James had been taken home by his care assistant after a trip out. Nell received a phone call to say her house was on fire. She arrived back to find the fire brigade and ambulances at the house. She went into shock and was taken into hospital where she ended up in a cubicle next to James. Nell said she was so angry with him – he had deliberately set the house alight although she suspected that he had not intended to burn the whole house. But she also recognised that he was angry with her:

> I think because his dad had died, I took someone else into my life which I shouldn't have done. I was there for James but not as much as he thought I should be. Then I had a heart attack…and then I wouldn't support him with this issue at the day centre and go and fight everybody and go and tell them that, you know, he can hit people if he likes

Nell continued her story of this incident. She was told she could go home from the hospital and take her son with her. Her response was to say: 'Where do you expect me to take him because I haven't got anywhere to go myself'. She said she stood her ground and left James until she had found herself accommodation whilst repairs were made to the house. She insisted that James needed help from a psychologist and that she wasn't going to risk taking him to a hotel if he was likely to set fires.

James was admitted to temporary accommodation and Nell talked with him about finding a place where he could live on his own, but near to her so she could visit. She described their responses to each other during this period: 'Poor James had his head in his hands and I did feel so sorry for him, but then [pause] I could see, like, if I'd have had him straight back he would have threatened me with that. Every time and every step of the way. And [pause] I thought no, this is wrong, we have got to get somewhere for him, just got to.' She found a halfway house belonging to the council's housing department that was in very bad condition and she was given £30 to decorate.

Nell recounted a further incident to demonstrate how she had sought to encourage James to be independent. Within a week of James moving in to his new accommodation Derek rang his mother to let her know that James was in hospital having got drunk and cut himself. Nell said she cleaned James up and said she was taking him out of the hospital – he wasn't ill, he had just got drunk and fallen over. She described how whilst she was living apart from him after the fire she had time to think about how she treated James: 'I knew that I could have died the day I had my heart attack and I knew that I would probably just pop off one day. And I wanted to [pause] really put James in a situation where he would miss his mum, but not his carer as such.'

When I interviewed Nell, James was living in his own flat near his mother. He lived on his own, but received money from the Independent Living Fund and had a carer coming to get him up, at teatime and to help him to bed. On Fridays someone took him to the pub. Nell said he was unable to walk and when he was inside he crawled on the floor. He couldn't do up a button nor communicate properly. But Nell described him as having tremendous spirit.

She described their current relationship as very strong although it had taken a long time to get where they were. She said he no longer allowed her to come and pick him up on a Sunday when he visited her for lunch because he knew she couldn't lift his wheelchair. Instead he came with Ring and Ride. Nell described him as more independent although if he was with 'silly people' he could be encouraged in the wrong direction. She said he played to an audience and could get himself into difficult situations where he could be vulnerable because he was too trusting.

I asked Nell if she thought James felt he was badly treated because of his disability. Her response was:

No, I don't – I don't think he does. Um, I mean not everybody likes disabled people. And, er, James does tend to dribble which can be very offensive to some people and I try and make him aware of that. Because if I hadn't been involved with disability I may not want to sit in a restaurant opposite somebody dribbling all over the place. But he can control it when he wants.

She also said she encouraged him to be aware of the difference between the carers who support him because it is their job, and herself and his brother 'who would always be in his life'.

At the time of the interview James was 36 so Nell described herself as having been a carer for 36 years. She was 57. She said she still felt trapped by James. She thought that if it had not been for him she would have sold up and moved to Spain, but she couldn't possibly do that as she had to be 'on call' – James rang her every morning and evening, and whenever he had a problem. She continued to provide practical support, for example by attaching Velcro to the front of his shirts because he couldn't manage buttons, and kept a supervisory eye on the support he got from care assistants. She had discussed with Derek what she hoped would happen when she died and said that if she knew she was going to die her response would probably be to go out and buy 200 shirts and Velcro them to keep him going.

She reflected on her experience in the context of the expectations on women of her generation: 'You see in my age group there was a lot of pressure put on parents to look after their disabled children. There was an awful lot of pressure and no help. And no future planning, never planning for this person to let go. You never had any dreams or aspirations of them actually letting go.' Nell told me she did not feel she could negotiate with James that she could move away from him because everyone else had disappeared from him – his father had died, and his brother Derek had moved away to be near to his wife's family. She thought James knew that her life was shaped by him and: 'He knows he is totally dependent on me, in a way. Which can't be nice.' But she also said 'He is a very warm, loving person. I mean if he rings me and I am out and I am on my mobile and I am in Sainsbury's, I mean people must wonder who the bloody hell I am talking to because, "I love you too, yes OK, love you lots, bye". They must think I have got a lover somewhere, you know.'

I invited Nell to reflect on what impact being a carer had had on her. She talked about her involvement in carers' groups and said she could see the changes that had taken place as a result of her and people like her fighting the system. She thought without this carers would still be frowned on as idiots and 'just a mother'.

Key issues

- Nell's story demonstrates the moral dilemmas that are often associated with caring, and the judgements that carers have to make about what is 'the right thing to do' in particular situations.
- Her account highlights the importance of understanding how care-receivers respond to the situations they are in, but also of care-givers being aware of their own needs for care.
- Nell was very aware of James's rights to take part in activities other people of his age would expect to be involved in, and saw it as her responsibility to help him achieve these rights. To this extent 'care' and 'rights' come together in Nell's account.

Caring in context: biography and identity

Although I invited carers to start by telling me about their lives before they became carers, this part of these interviews was very short. Indeed Nell started by saying she could not remember life before caring and spoke hardly at all about this period of her life. I coaxed Rose and Violet into talking a bit about their early lives, but it was only

Pauline who spoke more extensively about this without much prompting – although even she did not go into great detail. In the case of Barbara, her caring experiences had started well before the time she started caring for her son, the focus of my conversation with her. For Rose and Nell in particular, becoming a carer took place at the point at which they were starting to create their adult identities in cultural contexts which placed considerable emphasis on the family. Becoming a mother was expected and assumed, becoming a carer was unexpected and had a considerable emotional impact as well as disrupting the expected trajectory of the life course.

Most of the adult lives of these women were bound up with being a carer. That had had both negative and positive impacts on their sense of self. Nell spoke about her response when her husband died:

> I got James living with me and you think who on earth will want me with this baggage [pause]. Because everybody who is left on their own has got baggage, but not sort of quite as much. And you under-value yourself. And you accept any rubbish.

But later she spoke of her successes in raising money to get resources for disabled people:

> Now I feel good when they come up to me and they said as much, that was wonderful. And I do feel a sense of achievement, and I wouldn't have done that without James.

For Nell, Pauline and Violet the experience of being 'perpetual parents' (Settersten, 1999, p. 96) had meant that they were experiencing time and ageing rather differently from most parents; Barbara could anticipate something of this, whilst Rose was living with the uncertainty created by potentially life-threatening illnesses.

Pauline made a conscious decision to become the mother of a disabled son. This decision was made in part because of a sense that she and her husband 'had something to give'. Her account focused on the many challenges she faced in negotiating with professional agencies and both this and the considerable difficulty she experienced in her relationship with her son, and in managing his relationship with his father, defined her life for over twenty years. At the time of the interview she had reached the stage at which she was no longer sure that she wanted this to continue:

PAULINE: ....now I think, um, there are other things as well. You know, there is more, um, enjoyable things, yes.

INTERVIEWER: Things for you?

PAULINE: Things for me that I really enjoy doing. You know what I mean, Hobbies or whatever. You know, and people that—they wouldn't know what a carer was if you told them, you know.

Since Gloria became disabled rather than being born disabled, for Violet the transition to motherhood and 'becoming a carer' did not happen at the same time. She also came from a culture in which it was taken for granted that families would provide care for disabled relatives and so she felt little dissonance between motherhood and care-giving. Her religious beliefs provided another important dimension to her sense of self. Barbara had a clear sense of herself as a carer virtually throughout her life, although early in her account she suggested this was as much about others' perception as her own sense of self:

And that's when it started. They started pushing me into child care etc., etc., caring for people. I cared for my mother who had cancer, I cared for my father

Her own disability had given her an added insight into care-giving and receiving and, like Pauline, she too had experience of paid work in this capacity, but had not found this an entirely positive experience.

All of these women's stories illustrate the way in which their identities as carers are bound up with their identities as women. Early on in her narrative, Nell referred explicitly to gender expectations shaping her early marriage and motherhood, and Pauline's account of having to act as peacemaker between her husband and son (and then get the dinner after a day at work) is a clear example of the emotional labour involved in being a wife and mother.

The five mothers were at different stages – not just in their biographical life cycle, but also in their subjectivity regarding caring. Rose was obviously at an earlier stage than the others, as Surya was only seven. She was living very much in the present and did not dare consider the future because she was afraid her daughter might not survive. Barbara was 'facing the next challenge' and assuming a future in which her son would continue to need support, but would become more independent. Pauline was on the verge of giving up (although she did not say so explicitly) and was starting to distance herself from the carer identity. Both Violet and Nell had achieved an equilibrium in their relationships with their adult children and in their sense of self.

All these women were involved in carers' groups and spoke of the benefits they had received from sharing experiences with others and learning from them. Some were more self-consciously activists with a broader conception of campaigning for carers in general. Nell in particular had not only asserted her own rights in a range of situations in which she had found herself, but had acted as an advocate for other carers, had contributed to what she saw as a transformation in the way in which mothers of disabled children are viewed, and had somewhat surprised herself by developing skills in negotiating with policy makers and service providers at all levels in the system.

CHAPTER 4

Sons and Daughters

The role of carer for a disabled child can be understood as a particular type of parenting, albeit one that often continues well beyond what might usually be expected. But the origin of the carers' movement in the UK can be located in the experience of adult children caring for their elderly parents (see M. Barnes, 1997a, chapter 5). The circumstances of adult children supporting elderly, ill or disabled parents became a matter of particular concern – both because of the personal and social impact of the expansion in numbers of people in that position, and because of a perceived reluctance on the part of adult children to fulfil what could be regarded as their responsibilities to their ageing parents.

In this chapter I tell the stories of one son and three daughters who provided care and support to mothers and fathers at different stages in their lives.

ALAN'S STORY

Alan had cared for his mother Catherine when he was a child and she used to drink heavily, and later when she lived with him in the years before her death. She had a form of dementia at this stage. He lived on his own when I spoke to him.

Alan started his story by reflecting that it was only when he had made a purposeful decision to look after his mother in her final illness that he realised that this was not the first time he had done this. He then spoke about his childhood. He was the youngest of five children – he had a brother and three sisters. His father Michael was half Irish and half Lithuanian Jewish, whilst Catherine was from an Irish Catholic family. He said his parents' marriage was not a happy one – he described his mother as being jealous of her husband's relationship with his daughters. Neither Catherine's parents nor her parents-in-law liked her: 'But so [pause] what she always tried to do with me was to gain my sympathy and empathy of how badly she was done by everybody. But that was always either through, ummm, when she was drunk. She always drank. I remember all this drinking, always having the smell of drink on her.'

Later in his life she told him that drinking was the only way in which she coped with the difficulties and disappointments in her life: ten pregnancies, six live births and five live children by the time she was in her mid-30s, a loveless marriage and parents who didn't like her. Catherine worked nights in a hospital. Alan said he never knew when he came home whether she would be nasty through drink, when she might clout him, or whether she would be 'lovey dovey'. Alan (at nine or ten) learnt: 'to get your mother up off the bathroom floor, you learnt to, when she had passed out, make sure that she wasn't sick and make sure that she was lying and undressed and put her to bed'. He washed and bathed her when she was drunk and got her ready to go to work. He said neither his father nor his older siblings would do any of these things. But he said he also challenged her and told her that her behaviour wasn't acceptable. There was 'a lot of emotional stuff' and at times he literally stood between Catherine and Michael when they were arguing.

Alan talked of his mother's response when he started exploring his sexuality and she discovered this included a homosexual dimension: 'She was always very nasty about that.' He said she would brag about him to others but would never give him any positive feedback directly. When he got his A-levels his father: 'told me to leave home as soon as I could and not to come back. And I at first thought that was rejection. But I later realised it was about me getting away from her, is how he saw it.'

Alan embarked on a career that included nursing, mental welfare and social work. He married a woman who worked in similar areas. He talked about how he tried to encourage his parents to get on better, but Michael spoke of his concern about Catherine's drunkenness and how she was making 'all sorts of suggestions about his relationship with his daughters'. Alan said his sisters knew she was talking in this way and decided not to have anything more to do with Catherine.

Michael died from a heart attack when he was 54. This followed a row and a fight between him and Catherine. Alan described the funeral: 'My mother was very dramatic. And...this enormous black hat, God knows where it came from, but it was, like, just so out of place and out of character and not what the family was about at all, but everything had to be done. And like you know she stood at the side of the grave and tried to jump in the grave. And you know she had had a few drinks before, anyway.'

Alan said after Michael's death Catherine would sometimes ring him when she was drunk and say she was going to commit suicide. He wondered whether he should drive to see her (she lived about 100 miles away), but the next day he would phone her and she would have forgotten she had called him. He recounted Catherine's deteriorating health problems after Michael died. His brother and two of his sisters moved overseas and, seven years after his father's death, Alan divorced. Alan described his mother's reaction to this as 'trying to wheedle her way back in' by offering to provide money or support for him. His response to this was: 'I said you don't need to do that, if you need help I will provide you with help.' Catherine started to become ill but it was unclear what was wrong with her. Alan said she had always made a fuss about her health problems, but this appeared to be different. She started to become forgetful and to fall. She had both hips replaced and shattered a shoulder blade. Alan described her initial response to this: 'She spent loads of time in hospital that she loved. You know she absolutely adored—she was being cared for and the nurses were giving her whiskey. You know this is general nurses who were smuggling in whiskey and I was saying to them, look, she needs to stop drinking.'

But then it became clear that her problems were not only physical and she changed from being a 'good patient' to a 'problem patient'. Alan said she became quite demanding, shouted and screamed and was no longer a favourite. He commented on the way in which reactions of nursing staff changed towards her but he told them: 'Look, you can't just see her as who she is now. You've got to understand what's happened to her. You know, widowed relatively early, unhappy marriage, but what else has she done?'

He realised his mother had early stage dementia: 'And it was at that stage that she asked me to promise that she wouldn't go into a nursing home.' He agreed and found himself in negotiation with her multidisciplinary team: 'who felt that she should go into a nursing home because obviously as a bloke I wasn't capable of looking after her and did I realise what this would mean and all that sort of thing'. Catherine was not capable of moving back to her own home so Alan decided she should move in with him. 'I gave up my full-time career job and started to work independently with a view to knowing that if I was working independently I could devote more time to her'. The arrangements for her discharge and follow-up support were complicated because her home and thus the place where she was eligible to receive services was a long way from where Alan lived.

So in his 40s Alan was once again caring for his mother. He described how he started to look after her finances, having joint power of attorney with her solicitor. He negotiated with her to accept a cleaner who would also help her with her personal care and he provided physical care for her himself. He said his professional experience of working as a psychiatric nurse and as a social worker was crucial to his capacity to take this on, as was the fact that he was by this time living alone. When it became clear that living with him was going to be a long-term arrangement he knew he would not share the responsibility with his siblings: 'And of course my brothers and sisters, none of them wanted anything to do with her. None of them wanting to come anywhere near whilst all those negotiations were going on. And me not judging them for that because me knowing that none of them would have been able to cope with that.'

Alan said two of his sisters didn't see Catherine from the first time she was admitted to hospital until she died. His other sister visited Alan, but didn't go in to see her mother. His brother saw her three or four times during this period. Alan spoke about the way professional workers said how dreadful it was that the other children provided no support, but he told them there was a history to this. During this period, conversations with his siblings revealed more about their assumptions about family relationships. His brother said he did not understand how Alan had loved Catherine so much. Alan described his response:

> I said I didn't and that absolutely gobsmacked him. He thought our closeness was a mother–son closeness, you know, you love your mother, you love your son. And I said no, it wasn't about that. Our closeness was that she could have someone in the family who would guide her through things, negotiate her through things...What I was doing ...was keeping the relationship in the family going, to minimise the impact on my dad and of course then when dad died to minimise the impact on neighbours and everything else. So it looked like I was the doting son, it looked as if I couldn't do enough for her [pause]. But I didn't like her, and there were times when I hated her.

After Catherine moved in with him Alan didn't believe she would ever go back home. Nevertheless he kept her house going and on occasion took her there. He paid neighbours to look after the garden, keep the house clean and to air it before he and Catherine visited. Visits home were hard, as Catherine had to be persuaded she could not stay.

He described the impact of Catherine moving in. Physically it meant him moving out of his bedroom and re-arranging the way in which different rooms in the house were used. Space had to be found for zimmer frames, hoists, wheelchairs, continence pads, catheters, drips and other medical aids. Catherine couldn't move without assistance and had to be fed, taken to the toilet and bathed. But he said it was more difficult to deal with her dementia. She had a form of dementia that did not lead to steady decline, but where she retained some periods of lucidity. These were frightening times for Catherine, as she knew what was happening to her. Alan described the way in which Catherine sometimes confused him with someone else: if she thought he was Michael this was hard – he had to watch out and got lots of clouts whilst he was providing physical care for her. I asked him if it was a problem providing intimate care for her: 'We talked about it when she agreed to come and live with me. I said this will mean me physically caring for you, this will mean me physically bathing you, and I said are you okay with that, and she was perfectly fine.' He said having had the experience of working on female psychiatric wards, he knew how to provide personal care whilst respecting dignity, but he remained very aware that this was his mother and tried to ensure that he did not treat her like a child. This was particularly difficult when she became offensive or disinhibited and he had to tell her that this was unacceptable. He described how Catherine would squeeze his hand or tap him to indicate she had understood and he shouldn't keep going on. He said he was always aware that she was his mother: 'one of the things that I found was it was more like, you know, not taboo, but it was about trying to successfully constantly manage the fact that this was a parent who— the one thing I had always wanted from her was to be a good parent [laughter] and me having to parent her and her having to get into the child role and that was the bit I was always wary of'.

Alan said friends didn't visit whilst she was there and he was not able to have sexual relationships with people in his house. He used to adore going on holidays but when Catherine moved in he couldn't afford it. He couldn't relax over a long shower or even sit on the loo and read because he couldn't spend much time away from her. He described himself as always being tired. He learnt to sleep very quickly when Catherine slept.

Alan described his responsibility for 24-hour care for Catherine over four years. He drew on his professional knowledge and contacts to employ a pool of carers who worked shifts with him. A community psychiatric nurse (CPN), district nurses, a geriatrician and a GP had contact with her, but all the daily care was provided by Alan and the workers he employed directly. Alan described his role as the team manager. He said it worked well with the carers he employed but some medical staff found it a threat. He described different incidents that demonstrated this. For example, he had to convince the GP that Catherine had a physical problem with her ears when she was crying out in pain – the GP had claimed her screaming was a result of her dementia. On another occasion a locum nurse complained that Alan had sworn at her when he responded to her 'And how are we today' with 'I'm pissed off actually.' As someone who had worked in very similar roles he said he found himself very conscious of what professional staff were looking for in their response to his and

Catherine's situation. Whilst he wanted them to understand that lots of things had gone wrong for Catherine in her life he said he also wanted to preserve much of the family history as private so he didn't go into details about why his sisters didn't visit.

Catherine received a functional assessment, but Alan said there was no real needs led assessment of Catherine, nor of his ability to care. He described having to battle with the psycho-geriatrician in relation to his mother's medication when the doctor wanted to change this. This was an example of Alan asserting both his professional and personal knowledge to question a decision. He said this was something he had often done in his professional life, but on this occasion he was frightened that things would be taken away from him and his mother.

His personal response to looking after Catherine was complicated. I asked him if he felt resentful:

No, resentful is the wrong word really…I felt sad that I hadn't had a parent, a mother and that I was looking after my mother in her latter stages of life and I still wasn't getting from her the things that I would have wanted from a mother which was about recognition.

He had promised her he would not let her be admitted to a nursing home and he intended to respect that promise. He acknowledged that there was a certain amount of status associated with working in 'the business' and being a carer. He also said there were times when he could get her to laugh and enjoy things – she loved films, particularly Bette Davis, and 'you could put *Casablanca* on 100 times'. He described how Catherine sought to reconstruct her life:

she would say it again and again, 'I was a good mother, I worked hard and did my best for all of you.' And in a sense the thing about that was that I thought, you know she is not in a turmoil, 'cause what you didn't want to say to her was 'You were crap, your daughters don't come to see you because they hate you…' 'Cause she had a very strong ability to paint herself in a good light. And that was one of her survival techniques and I didn't want to take that away from her in any shape or form.

He said he wanted her to have dignity and maybe come to terms with some things. He described times in her final years when she would sit quietly and watch TV without a glass in her hand, when she would sit on a rug in the garden looking at the flowers and enjoying drizzle on her face, and when she would laugh when Alan swore in Spanish because she had told him off for swearing.

Catherine died at Alan's home. He described how he was alone with her, having called an ambulance after she had suffered an embolism. He had decided that if she died before the ambulance arrived he would not attempt resuscitation, but he felt awful afterward wondering if there was anything he could have done to keep her alive. For a while he also questioned whether he had looked after her properly and whether she would have been better off in a nursing home. Subsequently he said he had reflected a lot on why he took on the task of looking after her. He also said 'But what I have also learned to do is let other people care for me. Who maybe in the past might have tried, but realised it might have been a losing battle.' He said he used the experience and the learning from it in his professional life, though rarely announced that he had been a carer. He finished by saying that he had never believed 'the crap about professional distance' in work carried out by professional care-givers.

Key issues

- Alan's story challenges the inevitable association between love and care, but emphasises the significance of being prepared to take responsibility for another's well-being, of being attentive to others' needs as well as your own, and of ensuring that care-giving is 'competent', i.e. it achieves positive impacts.
- His account emphasised the importance of continuity between the values underpinning paid and lay care, and between personal and professional identities of care-givers.
- He identified the way in which 're-constructing' a narrative of a life can be important as a means of achieving an equilibrium that can be an important basis for a caring relationship.

SUSAN'S STORY

Susan was an only child who cared for her father, Geoff, after an accident left him with brain damage when has was 57 and she was 30. Geoff had died five years before I spoke to Susan. She had become a paid worker in a carers' organisation.

Susan described her family as close-knit. She was particularly close to her father who sometimes used to take her with him when he was working away from home. She described Geoff as having 'probably the best sense of humour of anybody I have ever known in my life'. She said they both loved food and shared the same sense of humour in relation to books and television programmes. She told me that after she married they continued to take holidays with her parents.

She had a daughter, but then divorced. She said her parents wanted her to move back home at this point but she wanted to maintain her independence.

She described how Geoff was hit by a speeding van whilst he was at work:

> it was his last job of the day. And he was hit by a speeding driver in a van. Now my dad as I said, was very, very tall and very, very big and the hospital said that if it wasn't for the fact that he had been so big he would have been killed outright, the injuries were so severe. But he was taken off [to hospital] and in a coma for six weeks. And you know subsequently it transpired that he had severe head injuries.

Susan said she blamed herself for the accident because Geoff had been very worried about her following her divorce. She said that people who worked with him described him as wandering around in a daze, and witnesses to the accident said he appeared to step out in front of the van in a daze.

Whilst Geoff was in a coma Susan said she and her mother took turns to sit with him and talk to him: 'It was an odd—I mean I had seen things on the TV but I never thought I would experience it myself. An odd thing where you talk to somebody who you don't know whether they can hear you or not.' She said it was difficult to arrange these regular hospital visits because she had to arrange childminders for her three-year-old daughter Amy. At weekends Amy used to go with her mother to visit her grandfather and read nursery rhymes to him.

Susan described Geoff after he came out of the coma. It was evident that the impact of the accident had knocked one of his eyes out of alignment. He remained in high dependency, then an ordinary ward for nearly three months and then was transferred into a specialist head injury clinic. Susan talked about her lack of knowledge about head injuries at the time, but then commented: 'I think I know everything there is to know about it now.' She described this as a particularly upsetting time as he and the other patients were locked in at night to prevent them from wandering off. On one occasion Geoff was found on the fire escape ready to jump out because he wanted to come home. She said he kept trying to persuade the doctors that he was well enough to leave and after a few weeks it was decided he could have a night home. Susan described what happened:

> Mum just couldn't cope, when the time came for him to go, all hell broke loose, and the police were there and it was really quite traumatic. Um, and he had to go to XXX and be sectioned [compulsorily detained under the Mental Health Act]. And it was like, this isn't my dad. He is a very intelligent, bright man. And going from this big teddy bear, pussycat of a man, he went to this violent, aggressive man and he had never been like that before. It was a complete personality change.

Geoff remained under section for a few weeks. Susan said she found the experience of visiting him hard. She had no previous experience of being in a psychiatric hospital and felt he was with people very different from him. He was finally allowed to return home and Susan described his condition at this time. Physically he had internal injuries and pains in his legs, but these did not prevent him walking. His head injuries had left him unable to see very well. But the main impact of the accident was on his behaviour. Susan illustrated this by recounting an incident when she went with him on a bus and he talked loudly about other passengers in a way that he would never have done before the accident. She said he also needed 24-hour support: he couldn't cook or prepare a hot drink; he couldn't shave, drive or go out on his own. I asked what help Geoff received at this time: 'In terms of support he never had the support that I think he should have had. It was as if [pause] we were just left to it then. He still had his appointments at the hospital, but nobody ever came to see him. Um, so we were kind of left really.' Susan said he was offered a visit to a specialist day centre, but no transport was provided so it would have meant a taxi to get him there. Her mother Mary had given up work. Susan was working but not earning very much and they could not afford a regular taxi fare. But she also said that Geoff did not want any outside help – he said his wife and daughter could look after him.

Susan described the way she and her mother simply accepted that they would not get any help: 'I mean now I would be very angry, but at the time we just accepted it, and we said, okay, right, this is what we are going to do.' Susan moved back to live with her parents and when her mother had to go into hospital she took a week off work to look after her father. She said they made sure that one of them was always available to look after Geoff. At this time Susan was working full time, studying, looking after her daughter and taking her turn to look after her father.

For a long time Geoff couldn't do anything for himself, but Susan said: 'even when he could, he still let us do it. Um, I think there came a point where Mum almost lost it. And I'm not surprised, it was extremely stressful and doing it seven days a week is a long time.' Susan said that after three or four years Mary told Geoff she would leave him. 'She said to me, I might leave the back kitchen door open tonight. I said why? She said, 'cause your father might walk out and not come back' [laughter]. Which we did laugh about, but there was an underlying seriousness which was quite worrying.' Susan admitted that at times she thought it might have been better if he had died in the accident, then would feel guilty that she was being unfair. But then Geoff did start to try to do things – like making a cup of tea or vacuuming.

Susan discussed her emotional response to what had happened to her father:

> And then there was this tremendous guilt because I would find myself spending more and more time at work and out of the house, and making excuses not to go back. Because I couldn't actually bear to see my father in the state that he was. Because that's not how he was before. We were very close before. But we—we were extremely distant at his death because I'd got nothing in common with him.

She said he couldn't read because it gave him bad headaches, he was indiscriminate in the television programmes he watched and she could no longer discuss shared interests with him. He couldn't cope with the noise Amy made and he used to shout at her as well as at Mary. Susan said she sometimes shouted back and there were times when she told him they would leave him. But she described herself as acting as a mediator when Geoff realised the impact he was having and asked Susan to tell her mother he never meant to hurt her. I asked her whether she felt what had happened was unfair:

> Yes we felt very unfair. I mean particularly as, um, he had always been a very polite, lovely man, and never would hurt anyone. He would care for his family, loved—he loved his family. He worked hard all his life, worked really hard. Provided us with everything. And it's like—there are so many horrid people wandering round this world, why does it have to happen to one of the nicest men?…I think we felt [pause] very, very angry

I also asked whether she thought Geoff had been angry. She said 'Yes I think he did, yes' and then went on to explain how none of his family ever visited him after the accident.

Susan said she moved back into her own house about six months after Geoff left hospital so that she could get on with her own life, because of the impact Geoff's behaviour was having on Amy and because of tensions with her mother. Susan felt Mary mollycoddled Geoff too much. Susan lived only 15 minutes' walk away and visited every day on her way to work. The only day she kept to herself was Saturday when Amy visited her father. Susan thought having this day to herself was essential because: 'I decided that I was becoming as nutty as a fruitcake.' She said her parents would visit for Sunday lunch but Geoff was uncomfortable being out of his house for long and wanted to return as soon as the meal was finished.

She reflected again on her emotional response, saying that she thought she had coped very badly at an emotional level with the impact of her father's accident. She illustrated this by describing how, before her parents came for lunch she would open a bottle of wine to have a few glasses. And one night a week when she and Amy used to stay at her parents' house she would also take some wine. She reflected: 'I know now that I should have sort of acted a lot more responsibly and just said, look, this is my dad, and put my feelings aside that I had, and just done it. But I know I found excuses not to do it.'

Susan described the final two years during which she was helping to care for her father as a time when he became more lucid and when it was possible to engage with him on occasion: 'Anything that he could moan about, he was quite happy you know…It was the only thing that sort of got the spark sometimes going and you can, you could sometimes see that spark come back.'

Susan's story focused on the impact of Geoff's accident on him, on family relationships, and on herself. She had little to say about services provided by statutory agencies because the only input they received was when Geoff needed a doctor: ' We didn't know there were supports for carers…We didn't know that, you know, we could get people to come and sit with dad when we went out. We didn't know we could send dad somewhere for a weekend while we had some rest. We just didn't know those things existed.'

About seven years after the accident (five years before I spoke to her), Geoff eventually died of a disease that could have been completely unrelated to his injuries. Susan described one way in which she responded to this: 'Dad and I had very similar views on death…And what we said was, if anything happened to us, we just go to the pub, you know…but when he did die they all [Geoff's family] wanted to come up and all the rest of it. But none of them was welcome…and then we went and we had the cremation, and then we went to the pub and Mum bought everybody in the pub a drink and then we went home to mine and I cooked'. Susan said she also knew he would have wanted his organs to be used for others. Organ failure meant this was not possible but Susan did agree to a post mortem in the hope that this might help improve understanding of the disease that killed him. She commented that: 'I didn't act appropriately in life, but in his death I made sure I did it right then.'

Susan talked about the impact of her experience with her father beyond his death She applied for a new post with a voluntary sector carers' organisation, describing her reasons for this as follows: 'by this time I had started to become aware of certain things, and I thought I would like to work for an organisation so that other people don't have to go through what we went through.' But the impact of caring for her father went beyond her decision to change jobs. She talked of weight problems and the psychological impact of the whole experience. 'I suppose, ummm, I get quite emotional. In a sense it's what makes me good at my job, it's also what makes me bad at my job. But I get very emotionally involved with my carers. So when I am on the phone with them, you know, I know exactly how they are feeling for the most part. And I cry with them, um, that's, as I say, good on one side, perhaps bad on another.'

Susan was continuing to support her mother who she thought had never really got over Geoff's accident and death. Susan noted that her mother had lost most of her previous interests and spent much of her time watching TV – as Geoff had done after his accident. Susan wondered what would happen when her mother needed support and anticipated becoming a carer for Mary some time in the future. The other impact that Susan identified was a panic response if Amy became ill. She said she felt unable to cope and found herself thinking what a terrible mother she was.

Reflecting on the absence of support available when they were caring for Geoff, Susan thought that respite would have been very valuable but problematic, as her mother wouldn't have left him. She considered that the experience had been a very isolating one for her mother, as she had no sense that other people had similar experiences. She suggested that if they had been able to meet and talk with others in a similar situation this would have been very helpful at the time and spoke proudly about the development of a befriending service for carers in which she is involved through her job. She finished the interview talking about the carers' organisation for which she worked:

from being a little organisation with £10 in the bank...we have got three services, £150,000 in the bank now. And it's still not enough for the services and support that we want to provide for carers in this city...you know there's 125,000 carers in the city and we've got nearly 400 on our mailing list...But you can't change the world overnight.

Key issues

- Susan's account highlights the psychological impacts on caring when this fundamentally disrupts the nature of the relationship that previously existed. But Susan also looks for continuities in that relationship and the values that underpin it.
- She demonstrates how responsibilities for care are often taken for granted – not least because no other option is available.
- Her account reflects on the importance of caring for oneself as well as the other person, but also the guilt or 'moral dilemmas' that can arise from not providing absolute dedication to the other.
- Susan's decision to work for a carers' organisation is a clear example of the way in which the personal can influence the public in terms not only of the roles people adopt, but also the way they carry these out.

BRIDGET'S STORY

Bridget had been involved in caring for various members of her family, but the focus of my interview with her was care for her mother Anne who had both cancer and Alzheimer's disease. Anne had been in hospital and in a nursing home and had died before I met Bridget. Her story also recounted her own experience of mental health difficulties.

Bridget told me about her early years in a small village in Ireland. She was the oldest of eight children – six boys and two girls, and her father's brother lived with the family. Her father's sister lived 13 miles away and Bridget said when she became ill they cycled to see her to look after her whilst she was in hospital. She described 'care in the community' as 'automatic' – in the village as a whole. She said she never really had a childhood as her mother was always having another baby. Her grandmother would come and look after her mother and the new baby, whilst Bridget worked on the fields and looked after animals with her father, as well as looking after her siblings.

In the late 1950s Bridget and her parents moved to a large city in England. Bridget described this move as a big culture shock. She told me that within five years of the move she had married, but this was not a happy marriage as her husband used to hit her: 'And at the time, now thank God women have great back-up systems and great help. At that time, absolutely nobody wanted to know, it was a very difficult time altogether.'

Bridget spoke of having been in a psychiatric hospital and when I asked her about this she told me she had experienced postnatal depression after the birth of her first child. Her husband had her committed to hospital where she was given ECT (electro-convulsive therapy). She said her father tried to get her to leave her husband after the birth of their first child, but Bridget thought she had to give the marriage a chance and stayed for five years during which time she had three children. She described health problems that resulted in major surgery and said the combination of this and her husband's violence caused long-term internal damage. She also spoke of her difficult divorce involving battles over custody of her children.

Bridget described how other members of the family followed her parents' move to England, including her mother's uncle Gerald who had had a stroke. The family bought a house for Gerald close to where they lived and Bridget said 'we were caring again'. She described how her mother, another niece and Bridget herself were involved in looking after her great-uncle. Because she was the eldest she was expected to do more than her siblings. Her job as a medical secretary in a primary care practice also gave her the flexibility to be free during the middle of the day and to work late.

Gerald was paralysed down one side as a result of his stroke. Bridget described him as a very finicky man. He had been a university professor and he still liked going to lectures as well as to the theatre and concerts. Bridget said she helped him get about as well as dressing him, doing his shopping and sometimes reading to him. But she also reflected on how Gerald would also read to her children as well. She described him as being 'extraordinarily good to my children' and teaching them a lot.

She talked about the attitude to her great-uncle when he was admitted to hospital and described this as 'very old fashioned'. She said there were strict rules about when people could visit and he was looked after by unqualified staff. So they took Gerald back home until he died.

Bridget's father developed dementia and was in hospital on and off for some time. When he died Bridget described it as a terrible wrench, as she thought he would live for ever – 'he was a very gentle man'. She then told me a bit about her mother's history. She described her mother Anne as a difficult woman. She had married from a 'very big farm' into a 'small farm' and felt her family should make up to her for the sacrifice she had made. Anne had been the youngest in her family and had only the equivalent of first school education. Her older brothers and sisters had gone to America from where they sent back beautiful things for her.

Anne expected her children to do whatever she asked them to. Bridget said when she had children her mother tried to tell her how she should look after them.

Bridget told me that Anne was diagnosed with cancer and subsequently also with Alzheimer's disease when she was 77. She had been living in sheltered accommodation after having sold the family home after her husband died. She was admitted to hospital following the diagnosis of cancer. Bridget described how she had been aware of her mother becoming forgetful, but also said that she was underhand in her dealings with her family so it was not easy to tell precisely when her behaviour changed. Bridget said: 'We didn't see eye to eye for years, but in the end we were closer'. Anne was discharged from the hospital into a nursing home: 'And I would go out most days and wash her and change her [incontinence] bag, and take her down into the big lounge.'

Bridget paused in her story of looking after her mother in order to recount a terrible road accident in which one of her brothers was injured and her nephew was killed. She described how she was called to the hospital to see her brother Joe, and when she was there was asked to identify a young man who had been killed in the accident. She went with the priest she had called to anoint Joe. Bridget had to identify what was left of her nephew Matthew's body. She had been very close to him and her detailed account of this event emphasised how awful this experience was. She said she had to arrange for Matthew's body to be taken back to the family home in Ireland, but because so little of his body had survived the accident she did not know how they would cope with preparing his body to be viewed by the family in his coffin.

During this horrendous experience Bridget said her mother was 'playing up'. 'Yes, she wasn't going to the funeral, then she was going to the funeral. We shouldn't have told her, then we shouldn't have taken her'. Bridget said she found it hard to deal with her mother's 'impossible and impractical' behaviour at this time.

I asked Bridget about the care she gave to Anne whilst she was in the nursing home. She explained that there were times when she would visit the home and find that her mother had not been dressed or she wouldn't be able to get up, so she felt she had to ensure Anne was washed and dressed: 'she probably would say to them to go away and come back next week or something'. But she also described taking in nutritious drinks for her mother, and finding them in the office on a later visit. So she made sure she gave them directly to Anne.

Bridget talked about her brothers who would visit to take their mother out: 'in order to get into mummy's good books, so they would get the money and the bond and all that'. But she said: 'I didn't feel anything because it was [pause] automatic that I would do it.' She described getting cross with Anne sometimes because of her behaviour. Bridget recounted one occasion, when Anne was still living in sheltered accommodation, when she visited to find her mother sitting in the dark without any heat. Bridget said she challenged her mother on this – she was not short of money – and Anne responded that her 'nerves were bad'. To which Bridget retorted 'Well at least you've never been locked in a mental hospital like I was.' She said she never knew what sort of mood her mother would be in when she went to visit and whether Anne would know who she was. Bridget described how her mother would talk about family members, and she would have to tell Anne that they had died, so Anne said they must say a Hail Mary for them. She also talked of the emotional demands of caring for her:

> she wouldn't wear pink socks, she wouldn't have this, and I said right, fine, we will find something else for you to wear. I had it very hard. And then it would be time for getting back and she – all old people do it – they pull at the heart strings: 'I am going home with you' and I go, 'How are you going to come home with me if your feet are all swollen, you can't even stand up.' You know.

I asked Bridget whether she ever felt that she had to get into any battles with staff about the care Anne received. She replied: 'I would knock near the edges of things, but I knew that if I pushed it too far, that they would take it out on her...and in her saner moments I can assure you, she was well able to fight her own battles [laughter]'. She also said the staff liked to see her coming and spending so much time with her mother.

Bridget's story once more took in other events that affected her life. A fire in her house destroyed many of her possessions and at the same time an elderly man who lived near her and had worked for her as a gardener died. Bridget was responsible for arranging his funeral.

Bridget described how in her last days her mother could hardly see and used to call out for *her* mother. Anne was eventually admitted to hospital where she died three days later.

Bridget concluded the interview by reflecting on the importance of cultural awareness in the care provided for Irish women and older people. She spoke of her experience in hospital when she gave birth, when appropriate attention was not given to modesty and dignity – she said she was wheeled along a corridor wearing only a pyjama top. When I spoke to her she was working with organisations concerned with Irish older people and with an Irish Mental Health team trying to ensure culturally aware services for Irish people.

Key issues

- Bridget's account of caring for her mother was interwoven with other stories of her life – caring was not a distinct and separate 'phase' of her life.
- Her own experience of both mental and physical health problems demonstrates her own need for care and the impact of an absence of care within her marriage.
- She felt the need to 'supplement' the care her mother was given in the nursing home in order to ensure that this was competently provided.
- Her experience emphasised for her the importance of being attentive to cultural issues as well as physical needs.

GINA'S STORY

Gina was caring for her mother Irena who lived with her. Irena had been born with dislocated hips and her health had deteriorated during time in refugee camps in Siberia in the Second World War and then in Africa. The family had arrived in England at the end of the war.

Before the interview Gina had told me her mother was recording her history in order to document the difficult times she had lived through. She told me something of this during the interview, occasionally checking with her mother who was also there, but who spoke very little English. Irena was born in Poland, the eldest of five children. She and her family were taken to Siberia in cattle trucks during the war. Her father eventually managed to get them out of the country and they became refugees, making their way via India to what was then Southern Rhodesia (now Zimbabwe). Gina described her family as very resourceful – whilst many died in refugee camps they survived. Irena's health had never been good; the horrific conditions in Siberia had made this worse, and then in Africa she contracted malaria and dysentery. Gina told me that Irena married a Polish man at a civil ceremony in India and that she was born in Rhodesia. This meant she was a British subject and at the end of the war the whole family was able to come to England – once more as refugees.

Gina was three or four when her family – Irena's younger siblings, her mother and father, her husband and Gina – came to England. Gina said they were very poor, but managed to get enough money together to buy a small house. Irena and the older sisters worked in a factory; Gina and her youngest aunt went to school where Gina started to learn English for the first time. Eventually they moved to another town where there were more work opportunities and a Polish community.

Gina explained that her parents had to take what work was available – her father worked as a dental technician and for a sweet manufacturer. She said her mother had wanted to be a doctor but that was never possible. Gina's sister was born in England (13 years younger than Gina). The family continued to speak Polish at home, but Gina went to an English school, as well as to Brownies and to Guides.

I asked Gina whether her mother's poor health meant she had to help out in extra ways when she was a child, but she did not think that was the case. She said: 'No, to this day really, although I am my mother's carer, I must tell you she cares for me more than I care for her. I mean I care for her very much, I care for her but she is my carer. She has always been there. My mother has always been there.' Gina said that financially things were hard, but her father was very careful about money and they led a very frugal life – they didn't have a car, didn't smoke or drink and Irena made clothes for the children. But they were prepared to spend money on their children's education. Gina described her mother as 'the guardian of the house'. She looked after the finances and kept detailed records of everything that was spent. Gina emphasised the way in which after their daughters had left home, her parents continued to be very careful with money but also offered them financial support when they needed it, and in doing so were scrupulously fair in terms of ensuring the same level of support was provided to each.

Gina spoke little about her own life but told me she left home when she was 18 or 19 and married at 23. She had various jobs – she said she felt most comfortable working with her hands, but also enjoyed writing for children's newspapers. She described enjoying independence after leaving home – buying her own shoes and clothes and being able to be adventurous in the sort of clothes she wore. Gina had four children, one of whom died when he was three days old. She spoke very little about this. She told me her sister Helena also married and had two children, one of whom was disabled. Gina said that Irena helped out financially to enable Helena and her husband buy a bigger house that could be adapted for her son. Gina also helped out with this. She said she and her husband divorced after about 12 years of marriage. She told me that her children had all attended university and had good jobs.

Gina described how Irena's poor health meant she was often in a lot of pain and eventually she became unable to walk other than round the house. Irena's husband looked after her and Gina popped in every day to help out. Gina told me what happened when a neighbour told them about attendance allowance: 'Now my father was a beautiful man, he never swore, he was a very religious man, he never told lies...when he filled the form out, my father wouldn't put anything embarrassing down. He would say, oh yes she can do that, oh yes she can do this, you know. But consequently attendance allowance wasn't given.'

Gina said her father's health was deteriorating by this time as well. He had had frostbite in his legs during the war and this had affected his circulation. Gina checked with her mother and then told me he also had pneumonia. She described how he was admitted to hospital on three occasions and each time was given the last rites. Eventually he died suddenly and peacefully one morning after returning from the market. Gina said: 'And of course my life changed completely on the morning my father died. I had to leave my house and I had to go and live with her.'

Gina told me that one of the first things she did was to arrange for her mother to see a specialist and have an operation she needed, but that would be difficult to perform because of the immobility of her legs. This was successful but Gina described it as a horrendous time for her mother – she was in severe pain, although Gina said she never complained. With the help of her doctor they applied once again for attendance allowance – this time successfully and backdated for two years. Gina described how this opened up other opportunities: Irena was given a wheelchair and her house was converted.

I asked Gina what she felt about having to wait so long for help they were entitled to. She replied '[We] didn't know what we were entitled to, nobody there really to advise us...A neighbour told me about the attendance allowance, a neighbour told us about going to the neighbourhood office and she said there is a carers' group there.' Gina said it was through contact with this group that they got access to practical help such as electric blankets and fires. The carers' support worker also told them they could get financial help from the Social Fund to pay for her father's funeral and that they could get help with adaptations to the house. But Gina also spoke about a lack of real concern to ensure that adaptations were carried out appropriately: for example, a spy hole put in the front door at eye level for a tall man, and 'A job that should have taken six weeks was about 13 to 14 weeks...And er, you know, the things were wrong and they kept coming back. One of the electricians started, another finished. And then after they had all gone, we found cigarette butts under the carpet.'

At the time of the interview Gina said she hadn't worked for some years. She received income support and care allowance. Her mother's attendance allowance enabled her to run a car. She made many clothes and household linens and sometimes sold things she had made. She described things as a struggle financially and said that finance was the most difficult issue for her. Whilst day-to-day expenses were covered, she worried what would happen if there were a crisis. Gina said that she and her mother had not been assessed for any other form of help apart from aids and adaptations, nor had she been assessed for her ability to support her mother. I asked Gina what help she gave to her mother:

> Well, my mum can't leave the house on her own, so I have to make sure that she has got a house that's warm. I have to pay for the electricity, the heating. I have to make sure that everything is safe for her. Um, things like doors, and er, I have to bathe her. I have to dress her legs every day. I have to put stockings on for her and take them off. I have to do a pedicure for her. All that I do for her. I do her hair, I cut her hair, perm it. I have done that for years. I get the pension, I do the shopping. I find out all the information. If she needs any equipment I am the one that organises somebody to come and see

But Gina also talked about what her mother did for her: 'although she is disabled, she is very resourceful. I came home one day, she had got a paintbrush tied on to the end of her walking stick and [was] painting the ceiling. She is that sort of person. She is a wonderful cook, she is a wonderful gardener.' Gina said her mum looked after her, as well as vice versa, and described her as her best friend, someone who was very funny and whom she could have a laugh with.

Through Gina I asked Irena what she found hard. Gina spoke to her mother, then said: 'Difficulty with walking, running. She is worrying not about her self...I mean I can hear her groaning sometimes, I know she is in agony...but she is worried about me and my sister, especially my sister. She knows I can cope.'

Gina talked about her involvement in a carers' group where she had used her craft skills to offer activities for members. She had also acted as secretary for a service users' group, but was finding it increasingly hard to continue with this as it took up a lot of time. She described herself as someone who found it hard to say no, but she was experiencing health problems so thought she needed to take a break from this. She had acted as a volunteer for Crossroads (a voluntary carers' organisation), was involved with Age Concern and helped support her disabled nephew. She spoke with concern about the fact that he would always need to be looked after, and about the financial impact on the family of the adaptations and care required for him.

Gina said: 'My mother doesn't like me doing it very much. She thinks I am gone too often. But I say to her, well, I have tried to put something back. And she said you have put more than enough back. But on the other hand if I was to stay at home I would go bad, wouldn't I.' She spoke with pride of successful campaigns she had been involved in – including the campaign for free TV licences for disabled people. Reflecting on their experiences of not knowing what they were entitled too, she was passing on information to others who were also unaware.

I asked Gina whether she ever felt things had been unfair. She acknowledged that sometimes she felt this, but suggested that they had been able to get help that many others were not able to do. She quoted the example of a 41-year-old disabled man who died from infection because he didn't know he could have a district nurse come to see the ulcer on his legs. She thought it important that people got information about their entitlements, but also that the way these are framed creates problems – for example, her invalid care allowance would stop when she was 60 – she was 59 at the time of interview. Looking to the future, she envisaged a time when she would need help with cleaning and when she might not be able to move Irena. She said Irena was determined to keep as active as possible so they were both worried what would happen if Gina couldn't physically help her. Gina said she would never put her mother into a home 'we believe in looking after the family all the time', but recognised that something might happen which would mean the need for further alterations to the house. She spoke of the way in which things can change suddenly and unpredictably. She concluded the interview reflecting on the hard lives that members of her family had had and the uncertainty of the future.

Key issues

- Gina explicitly acknowledged that care-receivers are also care-givers.
- She located her responsibility to her mother in the context of family relationships and the care her mother has provided for her.
- She spoke of 'rights' in terms of ensuring people have information about what help is available and being able to access this.

Caring in context: biography and identity

Parents of disabled children are usually young adults when they come to be in this position. Becoming a carer for a parent can happen at different stages of life – care-giving does not inevitably follow other events within a particular sequence within the overall trajectory of a life, and the duration of caring varies as a result (see Settersten, 1999, chapter 4). Alan was in this position when he was a boy and a teenager, as well as when he was in his 40s, whilst Susan suddenly found herself in this position in her early 30s. Both Gina and Bridget started caring for their mothers in middle age, but in Bridget's case this was not her first experience of being a family carer. Whilst the circumstances in which each of these four carers took on this role were very different, they all became carers when there were many other relationships and activities in their lives, and becoming a carer either radically altered how it was possible for them to live their lives, as in Alan's case, caused considerable re-organisation of their lives, as in Susan's case, or was described as one aspect of a whole complex of events and experiences that were shaping their lives, as in Bridget's case.

The nature of the relationships involved were very different and these stories demonstrate that family care-giving does not have to be the result of love. Alan's decision to care for his mother did not derive from what his siblings assumed was his love for her. In his case those qualities that have been characterised as constituting an ethic of care – attentiveness, reciprocity, responsibility, competence and responsiveness (see Chapter 6) – informed his personal and professional life from an early stage, but in a way that meant that his capacity to offer care was not restricted to someone he felt love for. In his case he saw no qualitative difference in his professional and personal identities as a care-giver and he recognised that in many different contexts 'the way I am and what I am and what I stand for' were tied up with his capacity to care. However, he was very clear that caring for his mother was very different from looking after the patients he used to care for in a psychiatric hospital. His experience of this was complicated by the fact that his care-giving made him more aware of what he had never had from her:

> Oh yes, very different. I was always conscious it was my mother and yes, yes it did feel very different yes. And it is about—I mean one of the things that I found was it was more like, you know, not taboo or—but it was about trying to successfully, constantly manage the fact that this was a parent, who—the one thing I had always wanted from her was to be a good parent [laughter]. And me having to parent her and her having to get into the child role, and that was the bit I was always wary of. So it wasn't necessarily the taboo about physicality, but it was more about being very conscious of 'Am I treating my parent like a child, rather than as an adult?'

In Bridget's case the care she gave to her mother was an expression of what she had grown up to understand family life to be about and her care for her mother was provided in the context of a difficult relationship. For Susan and Gina it was different. In Susan's case the sudden and dramatic impact of her father's accident meant that a very close relationship was transformed and she felt guilty that she had been unable to cope well (as she saw it) with this transformation. Whereas in many ways the relationship between Gina and her mother, Irena, was a continuation of a close reciprocal relationship which had existed for much of their lives:

> Not just my mum, she is my friend. And she is a nice mum, she is not a nasty mum. She is nice, loving, sympathetic, shoulder to cry on, helpful, generous, you know. And she is a good friend. And she is funny, very funny – we have a laugh.

Although her story suggests less disruption at the point of becoming a carer than Susan's and Alan's stories indicate, she also said her life changed completely at this point. But her account contained comparatively little about her own life and much of what she said about this was a result of my prompting. She was very keen to record the story of her mother's life because of the dramatic events she had been a part of. Her care for her mother was a way of affirming the value of her mother's life, but also appeared to be important to her own sense of self in so doing.

The individual histories of both parties are also important to an understanding of the circumstance and experience of care. I only have the stories as told by the care-givers, but their accounts give insights into the lives of their mothers and fathers as well as their own, which offer ways of understanding what the impact of being involved in a care-giving relationship meant to them.

Alan's story is unusual in the extent to which his public and private roles coalesced, although, as we have seen, a number of lay carers also work in paid caring roles. It is not necessarily the case that he went into paid care work because of his early experience of looking after his mother. But having developed a professional career as a paid carer he used his knowledge, skills and contacts to put together and manage a care package which aimed to integrate the best of paid and lay care. He acknowledged the 'street cred' attached to working 'in the business' and also being a carer, although did not trade on this by foregrounding his personal care experience in his work. The other three all became involved in carers' groups following their personal experiences, and in Susan's case changed jobs and became a paid worker working for a carers' organisation. All were committed to using their experiences beyond the personal sphere in order to achieve a better deal both for carers and those they support.

CHAPTER 5

Partners: 'In Sickness and in Health'

The final stories are those of husbands and wives who were caring or had cared for their partners as a result of long-term illness or dementia. The three people I spoke to were all elderly themselves and thus their stories offer reflections on long lives, spanning both good and bad times. Once again, although the primary focus of my conversations with them was the care they provided for a current or former partner, this was not necessarily the first time that they had been in a position of providing care and support for someone else. And, in two cases, the partner receiving care had also been a care-giver in the past.

DANIEL'S STORY

Daniel was caring for his second wife, Margaret, who had Alzheimer's disease and who had been admitted to a nursing home following a stroke. She was 86. His first wife, Joan, had died following an unexplained illness after 37 years of marriage.

Daniel's story started in the present day as he talked about what it was like for Margaret in the nursing home. He was often very upset as he recounted his story to me.

Daniel married his first wife in 1940. He told me that he met Joan at work and that he had worked for the same firm all his working life. He talked about being in the forces in the Second World War and having a lucky escape when the boat he was travelling on was torpedoed and he was picked up after abandoning ship. He explained that, because the firm they worked for did not employ married women, Joan left work just before they married.

Daniel described highlights of their marriage: 'We had a good life and so forth and we've always travelled. I had to go out to Australia in 1961 and I was out in Australia with the firm for four months organising a new factory, half a dozen of us went...but my wife had never been abroad. So I said when I come back we'll go abroad. They'd just started the package tours about 1961, 1962, so we went to Italy.' Daniel said Joan always had good health, but then developed a problem that was never clearly diagnosed. Joan saw a nerve specialist who at first thought there was nothing they could do for her. Later he said they could try a brain operation: 'so she had a brain op which was another trying experience because she had to have all her hair off and she'd got lovely hair. She came back and for about six months or more she wasn't too bad and so forth. I thought we'd won but then she had to go back into hospital and she died in the hospital.'

Daniel then told me how he and Margaret got together. Margaret had also worked for the same firm, although they had not seen much of each other over the years:

to put it bluntly she had a bit of a crush. She was single and at home with her mother, and she was the last one to stop with her mother until her mother died...when she knew she [Joan] was ill, she came up one day and she came into my office and said 'Could I help? While you're at work I could go and take her out and things.' So that's how it came about.

Daniel said sometimes he and Margaret would both take Joan out and then Margaret would come to help with Daniel's housekeeping. After Joan died Margaret continued to look after Daniel:

Eventually I said to Margaret I've decided I'm going to go to Norfolk. We'd always planned when we retired to go to Norfolk and I'm going to see if I can find a place. She said, 'If you like—' It was exactly like this, she said 'If you'd like, I'll come and look after you.

Daniel described how Margaret sold her house and they jointly bought a bungalow. Three years later he suggested that they should get married. They married in 1980 and had been married nearly 23 years when I spoke to Daniel.

Daniel told me about his continuing love of travelling and how he and Margaret took regular holidays abroad and visited friends in different parts of England. He liked Italy in particular and knew it well because he had also been there during the war. He also recalled that when he was at school he and two other boys were very keen on motorbikes. He said he was more interested in this than he was in girls at the time and was 20 before he really spoke to a girl. He and Margaret moved once more, but eventually decided to return to the city they had come from originally, to be close to Margaret's family and friends and to enable Daniel to receive treatment from a specialist.

Daniel told me that Margaret was diagnosed with Alzheimer's disease when she was 83. One of the first things he talked to me about was her experience of going to a day centre. He said she was always the last to be dropped off by the coach on her way back and this made her feel sick so he went to collect her instead. But: 'Southlands was a good thing because they kind of got talking together between themselves and so forth, which is one of the worst things in the nursing homes, that there's nobody to talk to except the carers who virtually only come, say a few words: "Do you want a cup of tea?" or "I want to take you to the toilet" and so forth, but there's no conversation.'

One of the impacts of Margaret's dementia was that this marked the end of their overseas holidays. Daniel told me their previous two holidays had been to the seaside resort where they had formerly lived: 'And the people there were marvellous. I told one or two of them, if they got a peculiar answer or anything from Margaret, not to worry. You know, she had a problem. They were that nice, all of them.'

Daniel said that as Margaret's dementia developed he paid for two people to come in the morning and the evening to wash and dress her and put her to bed. Then Margaret had a stroke and was unable to walk without assistance. A week later she was admitted to hospital. Daniel described how he went to visit her and saw her walking towards him along a corridor with her head on one side and her mouth open. He said he called a nurse saying he thought she had had another stroke and Margaret was taken for a scan. He told me the machine had broken down and they had to wait until the following day for this to be completed.

Margaret went into a nursing home (which Daniel was paying for) after she was discharged from hospital. He told me how he had found an organisation that helped locate vacancies in nursing homes, after the first home he identified was not satisfactory. He visited her every day, spending three or four hours with her, and described his impression of life in the home:

This is one of the reasons I stop with her. I take her down because they are all individual rooms with toilets, en-suite. Because otherwise she gets nobody virtually to talk to. She gets an occasional visitor from the church that we go to, but I mean normally when any of those people go they stop for half an hour and that's it. On the other hand, you see, probably there's at least 50 per cent in the home where she is that aren't able to talk. There's three lounges and I think that they could perhaps organise them better, to have people with like problems and so forth in one, and others in another

His impression was that the care workers washed and dressed Margaret in the morning, then brought her down and sat her in whatever chair was available, regardless of whether there was anyone nearby she could talk to. He said there appeared to be little activity in the home, in spite of a list of activities that had been set out in the brochure.

He described an example of a potentially restrictive care practice:

since my wife had the fall, they've got a small armchair...and the bottom seat slopes backwards, and it's so she can't stand up easily. And with her bed, because she'd had a fall out of bed some weeks back now, the matron asked me would I agree to her having her bed taken away and the mattresses put on the floor.

He then described Margaret's reaction to this:

the funny thing was that she didn't say anything about that. I thought she'd say. I had mentioned it to her like, I said 'They're going to lower your bed to stop you falling out and hurting yourself.' But of course you can't tell, when you tell people anything in that condition, sometimes they seem to take a bit in and sometimes they don't. I was surprised that she never complained and said 'Why haven't I got a bed?'

Daniel explained that he could not bring Margaret back home because he needed someone with him all the time if he was going to be able to move her. He told me he had asked his doctor if he knew any type of treatment which might help Margaret to walk, but he had said there was nothing that could be done as both her brain and her muscles had been affected by the stroke. Daniel said that Margaret did not receive any form of physiotherapy or exercise and there were few activities available for her. He described how he helped her when he visited:

When I go in the afternoon I take her various titbits. I take her these little trifles and bananas, different kinds of things. I take her pears after I've had them a day or two to ripen up a bit. I have to cut them up to give to her. I always take some lemonade, cold out of the fridge, and a small flask of tea. The first thing she very often says is 'I'm thirsty, I want a drink.'

He took drinks in for her because he did not trust the staff to help her drink when she was thirsty and said she had been admitted to hospital from the nursing home on one occasion suffering from dehydration.

Daniel spoke about Margaret's relationship with the care staff. She usually got on well with them and even if she couldn't remember who they were would smile at them. He said Margaret embarrassed him sometimes because she told him she loved him in front of the staff. Sometimes they joked when he arrived saying 'Here's your lover come now' which brightened her up a bit. But he also said Margaret developed an obsession that when he left home after visiting her he was going off to see other women. This upset him as he said the only women he had ever worried about were the two he married.

Daniel also spoke about the impact of this situation on himself. 'I've said to her many times 'I go home; I don't think anybody knows I'm alive actually. People that come, they come to see you here, nobody comes to see me. I'm there, by myself, looking after myself, cooking my meals and doing everything that's got to be done – the washing, the ironing. I have a woman that comes in to do the vacuuming and polishing one day a week, that's all.' He said no one had visited him to see if he needed any help and he had no contact with any carers' groups. He said he had lost interest in life and only kept going to look after Margaret.

He was upset when he talked about his loneliness and angry when he talked about having to pay for Margaret's nursing home care: 'So we were brought up to save for our old age, so we saved, didn't we, because that's the way we were trained. We worked, we saved, but the result of our savings is that we're taxed on the interest. People like me, I'm still paying income tax and I'm also paying on the interest and that. And because I've got savings I'm having to pay the full amount – £2000 a month is what I'm paying.' When I asked him if he felt this was unfair he said: 'I think it's disgraceful, disgraceful. Worse than unfair as far as I'm concerned. It's diabolical.' Daniel told me he had discovered that he could not touch Margaret's money because she had not authorised a power of attorney when she was still able to make decisions. He was worried that all his money would be taken up in paying for Margaret's care, but that her money could not be touched. He said he had spent a lot of time with solicitors trying to sort this out and was building up a big bill for this. He was worried that if he lived to be 100 he would have no money left to do anything with.

We ended our conversation with Daniel talking about how isolated he felt and his wish that someone might come to visit him to keep him company from time to time. I left him the number of the local carers' centre and suggested he could contact them about a befriending service.

Key issues

- Margaret had started out caring for Daniel's first wife, then for him. Their story illustrates that the identities of care-giver and care-receiver may change over time.
- Daniel was aware of the way in which Margaret responded to the care she received (e.g. brightening up when staff joked about her lover), but it was not always clear whether she shared his concerns, for example about the absence of activities.
- Daniel had a strong sense of the injustice of his situation, feeling that he had been let down by a welfare state which he had expected to provide support when needed.
- He also evidenced an awareness of an absence of care for himself, which left him feeling that his life only had value to the extent that he cared for Margaret.

EMILY'S STORY

Emily was living alone after the death of her husband Edward for whom she had cared after he developed dementia. During the course of her story it emerged that she had previously cared for her mother and that one her sons had experienced mental health problems and had disappeared without trace.

Emily told me a lot about her life over an initial interview and a follow-up visit. She was the eldest of four children – two daughters and two sons. Her father's civil service job had involved working in different locations so the family moved frequently. Emily said she had been living in the same house (the house she and Edward retired to) for 25 years – longer than she had lived anywhere else in her life. She had been to university during the Second World War to study mathematics. She then worked in a variety of posts, like her father, experiencing being sent round the country depending on where she was required to work. After the war she obtained employment in a scientific research establishment where she met her future husband. They started their married life living in accommodation provided by their employers, and two of their three sons were born there in the early 1950s. Edward was 12 years older than Emily and was 40 when their first son was born.

Emily described moving into the first house she and Edward had owned together in 1957. They had been saving, but had difficulty getting a mortgage because of Edward's age. Furniture and carpets were still difficult to get hold of after the war and they got what they could from relations.

Emily described her experience of looking after her mother. She said that after her father died neighbours told her that her mother wasn't eating properly because they saw her throwing her food out for the birds. Emily discovered her mother had problems with her sight and the food she prepared was always either under or over cooked so she threw it out. At first Emily visited her mother whenever the doctor said 'send for your daughter', but eventually her mother moved in to live with Emily and Edward. I asked Emily whether she thought she had any choice about this. She replied: ' I think you just feel, you just, er, I suppose I had more feelings of guilt than the rest of the family.' Emily described her mother as: 'ordering me around as though I was a maid in my own house'. She said her mother needed help getting dressed and was unable to get into the bath so they had a shower put in. Eventually she moved into a home near Emily's sister. She was later transferred into a nursing home where she died.

Quite early on in her narrative Emily told me what happened to her middle son Alastair. She said he went to university where he ran up big debts. He would spend all his grant as soon as it came and had to work during the summer holidays in order to earn enough to pay off his debts. Emily described him as 'like a bear with a sore head' till he had earned enough from his holiday jobs for this. After he left university Alastair got a job in the civil service. He lived not far from his older brother Richard and Emily said when she and Edward decided they needed to move somewhere less expensive after Edward retired they moved to be within easy reach of both boys. Emily told me Alastair lost his job after the department he worked for made a mess of an important contract, and he set up in business on his own. They saw him frequently because he would ring up and ask to come and stay for the night. But later Emily described him as changing – he was soon accusing people of all sorts of things, was running up debts and was 'in a state of collapse'.

Whilst his younger brother Michael was abroad Emily said that Alastair was collecting rent on Michael's house. The family hoped that he was earning enough from this and his consultancy work to keep going. She described how when Michael came back to Britain he went with his wife and baby daughter to visit Alastair, but got no answer when he rang the bell. Michael rang his mother who in turn rang Alastair's number and spoke into his answerphone telling him his brother was outside the front door – Emily said she knew Alastair would not pick up the phone until he knew who was calling. There was still no answer so Michael left. Emily said the next day she went to Alastair's flat where she found him in, but with all the curtains drawn and no food in the house apart from coffee and biscuits. She went to the shops and bought as much as she could for him, but the next day Alastair made it clear he wanted his mother to leave so she stocked up with food again and left. Emily said Alastair would not accept that he was ill. He kept running away and on the fifth occasion he did not return. Emily told me she had not heard from him since – in spite of trying to find out, she had no idea where he was.

Emily's narrative was not linear and interspersed with her story of Alastair she talked of her other sons' careers and Michael's marriage. She also spoke of Edward's family. She said he was the oldest child and he took on various responsibilities in relation to elderly relatives as the next of kin. She described how one of his aunts stopped eating after her husband died and was given ECT. Emily said she inherited money that she spent on clothes she never used. She had arthritis and followed a diet, but ended up not feeding herself properly and becoming depressed and incontinent. Edward and Emily used to visit to try to sort out her affairs, and when she went into a home it was Edward who took charge of selling her house. Edward was able to pass over his power of attorney to younger relative before his aunt died.

Emily described how similar expectations arose when Edward's younger sister had a stroke. She said he was 83 at the time and, as her next of kin, was consulted by phone about the treatment that was being proposed for her. She lived a long distance from them and Emily said she refused to allow Edward to go to the hospital to talk to the doctor after they had just returned home from visiting her. Edward by this time was in a state of collapse. Instead, two friends who lived close by persuaded the doctor to find a place for her in a local cottage hospital. Emily told me she also persuaded a local solicitor to encourage Edward's sister to pass on power of attorney to her two nephews who had been identified as her executors. Emily was adamant that Edward was too old to take this on.

Emily described their life together after Edward's retirement. They enjoyed taking holidays together, whilst Edward enjoyed going to concerts and industrial archaeology and she loved walking. They went everywhere by public transport. They had sold their car when Edward developed glaucoma, but Emily also demonstrated a commitment to public transport: 'I am fed up of standing on the road waiting for a bus and seeing every car go by with one person in. Nobody offers lifts to anybody else. They are all content to be in their own little box taking up space.'

Emily said that in 1994 she realised that Edward was starting to demonstrate symptoms of confusion, but that this developed gradually. She told me she decided they should do residential courses together to try to keep him active. During the second of these he had a minor stroke and was taken to hospital, but she was able to take him home the same day. She said this was the first noticeable stroke he had and it was followed by 'a dozen or more' before he died.

Emily spoke of the way in which Edward's dementia affected him: 'he didn't know me as a wife. He would say 'I've seen you before,' and 'I've known you a long time.' When his eldest son came to visit he said 'There is my best friend.' She also talked about the help they received. She organised a care assistant to visit him on a private basis. She was able to get someone from MIND (a mental health voluntary organisation) to come twice a week, but this was reduced to once a week when Edward went to a day centre for two days. She said the first person sent by MIND was a young man who shaved Edward. He didn't stay long as he got another job and was succeeded by two young women in quick succession. Emily spoke about the difficulty she had in getting the level of help they needed. She said that a social worker had to give approval for the care assistants. The first social worker had told her to get in touch if she felt she needed any more support, but when she did this she found the worker had moved to another office. Eventually another social worker came to see her and agreed she could have help to get Edward up on days when neither the private care assistant nor those from MIND came. Emily said she received help to get Edward up on four days a week.

Emily spoke in some detail about caring for Edward. She told me he often fell and she got used to picking him up and sending for ambulance staff to help her. She had to wash and dress him. The carers who came from MIND said it was not their job to get him up: 'if I had left him upstairs because he wouldn't get up for me, all she would do was let him move to the chair beside the bed. He became incontinent over night. She wouldn't change the nappy or anything like that. He would be sitting wet when I got home at midday.' Emily said after this experience she made sure she attended to this before she went out. She told me how she had to leave early from meetings of the University of the Third Age because it was not possible to negotiate the care assistant hours, so that three of the five allocated hours were provided on one day. She commented: 'You take what you can get, you see.' When Edward started to go to the day centre twice a week, the hours from the care assistant were reduced from five to three. But Edward gradually gave up going to the centre by refusing to get up when he was due to go.

Emily talked of taking Edward to daytime concerts – at first by bus, then by taxi and Ring and Ride. She said 'I could keep him happy with music. He needed to see me, he needed to see somebody that he knew...he wasn't happy left alone. He would be yelling "Hello!" I said, "I am in the kitchen getting your meal, I will be there in a minute." I usually had to appear to make sure that he knew.' But Emily described how when a new season of concerts was starting she was unable to get him out of bed to go and he never got up again for concerts. She said he became less co-operative so his days were spent 'Nine to nine downstairs and nine to nine upstairs'. Sometimes he wouldn't come down at all. Occasionally he would go to a day centre if transport could be arranged.

Emily described how Edward's sight started to fail and his mobility deteriorated. A physiotherapist came to assess him and suggested the steps to the front of the house should be altered, but waiting lists for adaptations to be done by social services were so long that Emily said she arranged for this to be done herself. She also bought a stair rail and Richard fitted it.

Emily's story detailed the way in which during the ten years she was caring for Edward he was gradually getting worse and she was finding it harder to look after him. Although his personality didn't really change she said on one occasion: 'He managed to hit me very hard on the ear. But I mean that was a rare event. He didn't become really violent in any way whatsoever. He was just mild. And you could keep him happy with music.' She told me she thought that at some point he stopped knowing who she was. They celebrated their Golden Wedding with a trip on a canal boat her son helped to organise, but she said she thought Edward did not know the significance of this event. Emily told me this was the last time he went away as he became incontinent overnight. Emily contrasted the experience of caring for her mother with caring for Edward – whilst her mother had got muddled she could continue to hold a conversation, but Edward became unable to answer her properly.

She said Edward continued to have more little strokes. As a result of one of these he ended up in hospital at 3 a.m. although he was discharged at 8 a.m. with the message that he'd be all right in 24 hours. As Emily said 'He was, I wasn't'. She said Edward managed to sleep it off, but she was awake all night. She described starting to feel unwell herself – she was occasionally sick and 'felt rotten'. When a doctor examined her he said there wasn't anything wrong – 'just stress...But he did take the trouble to come to the house one day, triggered by my daughter in law' and as a result of this visit he tried to get Social Services to provide more support for Emily, saying he wouldn't answer for the consequences if she didn't get more help. But Emily said there was little response to this. Emily told me she was looking after Edward 24 hours a day, seven days a week and having to get up three times in the night to see to him. She was told she couldn't get anyone to sleep in until she was getting up four times a night. But she also thought the fact that they couldn't be charged full price for the help that was being provided (because Edward's pensions and savings did not amount to much) also accounted for them not receiving more help. Emily noted that if she needed help if she became unwell again she would have to pay full price because now the house and joint savings were all hers. When I asked her if she thought this was unfair, she paused and then commented: 'You do feel that, um, er, if you have done any savings you are being penalised for it.' Emily also thought that Social Services were spending too much time discussing who they should help and not enough on actually providing support to people obviously in need. She wondered out loud if she would have needed to be admitted to hospital and have an operation at 79 if she had received more help earlier.

Emily felt she was 'always in a queue to see a social worker'. She told me after encouragement from a carers' group she wrote to Social Services, but it was six months before anyone came to see her. There was no assessment of her capacity to look after Edward: 'the last thing they were worrying about was me'. She said the only one who had expressed any concern about her was a health visitor sent by the doctor when Edward's health problems started to become evident. But she had retired and no one replaced her. The private carer that Emily had arranged was concerned, but Emily said she was a sick woman herself and she only worked for them on one day a week.

Emily resumed her story of what had happened to her: three days after Edward was discharged from hospital after being admitted with a chest infection she was ringing for an ambulance again – this time because she had vomited blood. She had developed an internal infection and was seriously ill – she told me the doctor said she could have died from this if she hadn't been so fit from the walking she had done throughout her life and from never having smoked or drunk alcohol. Emily said that whilst she was in hospital her sons and daughter-in-law organised a rota to come and look after Edward. The private carer and Emily's son Richard moved in for a week each to look after Edward. But Emily said the hospital was pressing for Edward to be moved into a nursing home so that she could be discharged and not have to look after him. He spent six weeks in a nursing home that catered for people with Alzheimer's disease. Emily did not think this was appropriate as he suffered from multi-infarct dementia and not Alzheimer's. She was unable to visit him there. Edward died whilst he was in the nursing home. Emily said 'When we moved in here [their house], he said I don't want to move again, I want to go out of here in a box. And I am guilty of collapsing first. He nearly killed me off, because they said it was only that I was a healthy walker that saved me. And I effectively killed him off'. She thought it was a pity that she could not have moved somewhere to convalesce and thus enable Edward to stay at home and 'die peacefully in his own bed'.

Emily criticised the amount of time spent by the local authority on producing Better Value reports, and the time spent by the National Health Service (NHS) on re-organisations, rather than thinking about the people they are meant to serve. She said some of the care assistants who visited her said they thought she had more needs than others they visited, but there had been no attempt to assess her needs. She had no relations nearby who could help out on a regular basis and no neighbours who were in a position to help. She thought she would have been much better able to continue to support her husband if she had received more help, but instead she was left feeling 'slightly guilty that I wasn't around to see my husband off, that he had to die in a nursing home'. Reflecting on her experiences of being a carer at different stages in her life she said she had just done what was necessary, but she did say that she had been annoyed that her sister and one brother had not helped enough when her mother was no longer able to look after herself.

Emily had some involvement with a carers' group because she thought it was important that such groups include people like her who had experience of providing 24-hour care when they themselves are elderly. She took an active interest in what was happening in relation to health and social care services. But she had returned to being an active participant in the University of the Third Age and regularly went on trips and to talks organised by U3A. Her health problems meant she was unable to walk as far as she used to do, but she still walked and enjoyed doing so.

Key issues

- Emily's account offers a powerful reflection on the importance of recognising the needs of care-givers to receive care.
- She illustrated how important it is to ensure that care can enable some continuity of interest and activity for care receivers. Emily knew Edwards' response to music was important in sustaining his well-being.
- Her description of the support offered by care assistants illustrates that effective care requires that caring work is competently performed.
- Her narrative of her life with Edward was interspersed with stories of her sons and of her own interests in, for example, family history and walking the canals. This demonstrated the way in which care-giving is interwoven with other aspects of everyday life.

LISE'S STORY

Lise had cared for her husband Eric after he had a stroke when they were both in their 50s. She had cared for him for 18 years until he died, six years before I spoke to her. Her story also reflected on earlier periods of caring for her parents.

Lise started her story by describing her childhood as the oldest of three children in an affluent German Jewish family. Her father was in business. They had servants and she told me her mother did little other than cook in terms of household tasks. At first Lise and her siblings were educated by a nanny. As a family they strictly observed Jewish traditions, which meant they would all get together for Friday meals. But Lise said she did not see much of her mother during her childhood and said she did not have much maternal feeling.

Lise told me something of what it was like to be a Jew in 1930s Germany. At school she said she was ignored because she was Jewish and her education suffered as a result. Her father was tied to a lamp-post and spat upon. But the family was tipped off just before Kristallnacht and her father left the house so he wasn't there when the SS came looking for him. Instead Lise said they took her ten-year-old brother, and her father had to sign over his business in order to get him freed. The family left Germany at night leaving everything behind them. There were 11 members of the family and business partners on the train leaving Germany, including a three-month old baby that Lise looked after.

Lise described their life during the war in England. They were given money by a Jewish organisation, but she said her father was interned when he first arrived, for checks to be carried out to see whether he was a spy. Lise's parents went to another part of the country where her father was able to work, leaving Lise and her sister to be looked after by her uncle. Lise told me she looked after her younger cousins; she was 15 at the time and was over school age, but didn't have a work permit so was unable to take on paid work. Later she joined her parents and did different jobs, including making chocolates and making cosmetics, until she eventually got a job as a cinema projectionist. Her wages were an important contribution to the housekeeping.

During the remainder of the war Lise and her parents lived in two rooms in a private house, where her mother had to cook in the bathroom. There were two beds for the three children. She described how her brother discovered it was sometimes possible to get coins that hadn't been used out of public telephones and this was a source of money to buy chocolates for the children.

Lise said that eventually the family were able to rent a house near to one her uncle had acquired. There were many Jewish refugees in the area who met in the house of a Rabbi. Lise described the creation of a German-speaking Jewish community in England based around this. The family spoke German at home, maintained the Jewish traditions and lived very closely as a family. Lise developed a relationship with a non-Jewish man and her parents were very worried that she would marry him. But Lise eventually realised she was 'too Jewish' to do that.

After the war she was offered a job as an interpreter with American forces in Germany. She told me she saw this as an opportunity to get away from her job as a projectionist, which involved working very long hours, and to get away from her boyfriend. But her parents were horrified that she wanted to go back to Germany.

Lise was in Germany for two years. During this time she met Eric. Eric had also left Germany at the start of the war. He had returned to try to find his parents who he later discovered had died. Lise and Eric both worked with American forces and were subject to some restriction of movement. But she also said: 'We used GI transport and went all over the place. For long weekends we went to Italy across the mountains. We did – it was probably the best time of my life.'

Lise told me she did not want to stay in Germany, but Eric did and when he proposed she initially said no because of this. Lise described this as 'the only time in my marriage when I put my foot down' – she insisted she was going to return to England and Eric said if she married him he would come with her. Lise said she returned to England before Eric so that he could gain qualifications. She herself studied on her return to England and qualified as a dressmaker. But a few weeks after getting a job she became ill. She told me her sister looked after her, but also wrote to Eric asking him to come to England because of her illness.

Eric and Lise started their married life living in one room, with a parti-tion to separate out a kitchen area and a bathroom so poor that they went to her parents' house to bath. As Lise started to recover she worked at her dressmaking at home. Eric was studying and was on a grant. She said: 'It was tough, it was terribly tough. We did save some money, but we wanted—we didn't want to spend that because we wanted eventually to buy a home.' Lise told me they were finally able to put a down payment on a house when Eric received a lump sum payment from East Germany because his parents had been killed before he was 18. Lise was clear she wanted to buy somewhere where she would feel happy to live for the long term. She told me they found a house she liked but which Eric thought was too expensive and he refused to buy it. Lise said: 'I didn't speak to him for a month!' and eventually Eric gave in and said they could buy it if they cut down on housekeeping.

Eric was offered a job which would involve going back to Germany for six months for him to learn the ropes. Lise told me she reluctantly agreed to this. Her response indicated her unwillingness to have contact with people who had associations with the Nazi era: 'I said, do we have to socialise, so he said to a certain extent yes, only with the head of department and people like that. So I said how old are they, because I was very reluctant to have dealings with my age groups. I didn't mind the younger age groups.'

Lise told me after they returned to England her mother was diagnosed with cancer and she gave up her dressmaking to care for her. She cooked, shopped, cleaned and provided some personal care for her mother. Her father also had cancer and when it was discovered how ill his wife was Lise said she and her sister decided not to tell him. Her mother died quite quickly when she was 61.

Lise described how after his wife died her father moved to Switzerland. She said on Eric's encouragement she joined him for two weeks. She visited again the following year doing 'more caring, more caring' whilst she was with him. Lise then told me that when she and Eric had collected her father from the airport to return to England Eric announced out of the blue that he wanted a divorce. He had met a woman through his work in Germany and he wanted to marry her. She said: 'The following day he rang and emptied our joint bank account. He told me after he had done it, that left me with nothing.'

Lise described her response to Eric leaving her: 'I told him after a week I'm not giving you a divorce. You can go and live with her – I can't stop you from that, but I am not divorcing you.' She said she still loved Eric and she did not want to live on her own (she was 48 and had been married for 24 years) and she was worried about being left with very little money. But she then described how at the same time the firm for which Eric was working was in difficulties and Eric lost his job. It was uncertain whether he would be able to live and work in Germany and eventually the affair ended.

Lise described how through her connections she managed to find an opportunity for a new job for Eric, which involved moving to another part of the country. She said Eric was resigned to staying with her and agreed to the new start that such a move entailed. Her view was that he had been looking for a younger woman: 'But I realised all that. I also realised that he was a very, very difficult man and if somebody, even if you try and find somebody they soon find out how difficult it was and they wouldn't stay with him. So he would have to stay with me. I still loved him. But by that time I was out for security.' She said he took up the new job, while she stayed to look after her father until he died six months later. On her 50th birthday Eric arranged a surprise holiday trip for her and she felt that indicated he did want to try to make a go of it.

After their move Lise continued to work and she kept the money she earned for her own purposes. Eric kept the house, paid the bills and provided her with money for housekeeping. She said he was generous with presents. But after four years of a 'marriage of convenience – but not a bad marriage' Eric suddenly had a stroke.

Lise described how in the immediate aftermath doctors thought he would not live. The doctors couldn't make him understand anything, but she told me she realised that he could understand German, but not English. She said that because she was the only one who could communicate with him she felt she needed to be with him all the time – she only went home to sleep. She described how after two weeks 'he had a bad turn, a very bad turn' and she was called back to the hospital. She said she insisted they call the consultant to see him, but the doctors were concerned about her as well as Eric and they called her GP to see her. He explained what was wrong with Eric, that he was on the danger list and could become unconscious at any time, but also insisted that Lise get some rest. Lise said for the six weeks that Eric was on the danger list she was at the hospital by 8 o'clock every morning. She was sleeping very little but refused to take sleeping tablets in case she was called in the middle of the night to go to the hospital.

Lise's story then recounted the impact of Eric's stroke on each of them individually, and on their marriage. One aspect of Lise's story focused on the financial impact of Eric's stroke and the way in which this caused a role reversal in terms of responsibilities for managing their affairs. Eric was not able to work again. Lise told me his union supported an application for a lump sum as well as a pension from the firm he worked for because the stroke was considered to be due to stress. She discovered that she could not get access to money from their bank account because it was not a joint account. Eventually Eric was able to sign an authorisation to give her access and control over their account. Lise said: 'In fact it's in one of his diaries, while I was still negotiating with the form, it says, my wife is going out today to discuss my future with personnel. Um, so this is the very first bank statement which I opened and showed him and he said it's none of my business any more, that's your business.' Lise said she was concerned that if he did anything that might cause stress he would have another stroke. She was worried about what might happen to them if they both needed to be looked after so she invested some money she had inherited to ensure financial security. She took up her dressmaking again so that she had an income. Lise also said: 'And then the other fear was while he was alive, what am I going to do if he dies before me…I find it extremely hard to live on my own.'

Lise told me Eric was not an easy man to care for. In the hospital he was sometimes rude to the nurses. He did not like Lise to leave him and he could be very critical both of Lise and carers who sat with him so that she could leave the house. At times he would shout at her and not let her out of his sight. She worked at home on her dressmaking and had to see customers in sight of Eric. Lise said she got tired and bad tempered and would have a go at Eric when he had a go at her. But she also said he would try to do things on his own – for example, she found him trying to get up the steps to the house on his own after she had taken him for a walk, and he would also try to feed himself, although there were times when he could not hold a cup.

Lise also talked about struggles to get the support they needed: 'I had to threaten the incontinence nurse whose home number I had. Because occasionally he was on a catheter. I threatened her unless I get pads I phone her in the middle of the night and you come and change his bed. I mean those were everyday happenings.' She also spoke of her indignation at being investigated to ensure she wasn't working whilst also claiming benefit: 'I said no, I am not asking for anything. All I want is my husband's invalidity paid. For which I am entitled…All I want is his, I think, £70 a week for which I am entitled.'

Her experiences led to her becoming involved in a carers' group. 'I thought, well if I can help somebody else not to have that struggle, and make them the way I was, stand on their own feet and not be talked down to.' Although she had never been involved in anything like this before: 'When I realised how unfair it was, when I applied for mobility allowance, they refused me, he couldn't even stand up at the time… I fairly quickly learned to be a rebel. I went straight to my MP.' She also got involved in helping other people in similar situations: 'an 87-year-old man who lives down the road. He had a spinal operation. He was in hospital and they wanted to get rid of him. They are going to give him a portable toilet and blaa, blaa. I said don't you dare leave your hospital bed until your lift is installed…they wanted to send him home before they put a rail up to go upstairs…I knew the rail would be at least six months coming. I said you stay in until the rail comes.' She also became involved in a group that met with social services managers to try to secure better services for people needing help at home. She described herself as becoming an expert as a result of her experiences of caring for Eric and having to do battle to get the support he needed. Much of the final part of my interview with her focused on her experiences of being involved in a carers' group and of trying to improve services.

Eric had died six years before I spoke with Lise. She had been caring for him for about 18 years. She said: 'Everybody thinks I am mad, I'd give anything to have him back. That sort of life, everybody thinks you must be

out of your mind, you had no life. But I had more purpose and more satisfaction than I have now.' She said she did not think of looking after Eric as
a burden, but as what her life had become: 'And for better or worse I take
it. But don't forget, having had so many knocks, from childhood onward,
you don't expect to have a life full of joys. I didn't.'

Key issues

- In Lise's story injustice is associated with not receiving entitlements.
  She does not distinguish fighting for her rights and Eric's rights.
- Lise's strong identification as a carer is interwoven with her sense of
  her self as fighting for her own and others' rights.
- Her early experiences as a refugee may well have affected her need
  for security and thus her willingness to fight to keep her husband
  and subsequently look after him.

Caring in context: biography and identity

The way in which personal biographies intersect with and are often
profoundly affected by wider social changes and significant events is
evident in the life stories of older people. These carers were in their
late 70s or 80s when I interviewed them in 2001 and 2002, and for this
cohort it is virtually impossible to tell the story of their private lives
without discussing in some way the experience of the highly public
event of the Second World War. For Lise (as for Irena and her daughter Gina) this time caused a major fracture in the trajectory of her
family's life courses, with fundamental consequences for where and
how she was able to live her life. In Lise's case her refusal to return to
live in Germany where she and her family had experienced persecution placed a tension on her marriage and provided the opportunity
for her husband to go there alone and to develop a new relationship.
His subsequent need for her support following his stroke was perhaps
the first time in their marriage that Lise had been in a comparatively
more powerful position within their relationship and she developed
important strengths in the course of this. In Daniel and Emily's case
the experience of war was considerably less traumatic and obviously
disruptive, but nevertheless significant. It can be seen to have created
opportunities for Emily to pursue and apply her education, whilst for

Daniel it helped instil a love of travel, as well as leaving him aware of his luck in being alive when many of his contemporaries were not.

The other significant public event associated with the postwar optimism and collectivism was the establishment of the welfare state in the UK. People of Daniel, Emily and Lise's ages had seen the establishment of the NHS and the introduction of a benefit system intended to ensure that citizens would receive the help they needed when they needed it, in return for the contributions they had made throughout their lives. When they sought to make a call on that system and found it wanting, they seemed to experience a more profound sense of injustice than was felt by those born after its establishment.

Caring for a spouse or partner may start before old age, as Lise's experience shows. But when a 'caring relationship' develops in the context of a marriage or long-term-partner relationship both partners have to negotiate significant changes in the way in which they have learnt to be together, and it can mark an end to hopes and expectations about how they may be able to share the final stages of their lives when other responsibilities (children, work) have lessened or been left behind. Daniel's distress in telling his story is one indication of the impact of this. It often also means that one partner takes on physically and emotionally demanding care work at a time when their own health may be deteriorating or a greater risk – as Emily found out.

Marriages and partnerships will often have included difficulties and conflicts as well as love and passion. Lise's marriage to Eric would have ended if she had not refused to divorce him, and she described him as being quite aggressive towards her whilst she was caring for him. She said people would ask her why she put up with this, but she said they did not know what came before. In effect she was saying that in order to understand the hows and whys of the caring relationship in which they were both involved it was necessarily to understand how they had got to where they were.

Whilst all three had a sense of the inter-relationship between public services and private care, Daniel's experience of care-giving had left him far more isolated than either Emily or Lise. He described himself as someone who was not really a group person and had not become connected with any groups associated with caring. One opportunity the interview afforded was for him to express *his* need for social contact. Throughout her period as care-giver to her husband Emily had sought to sustain her identity beyond this role – she had continued to take part in U3A activities whenever this was possible and to pursue her walking interests. She had become involved in a carers' group and in this context advocated in particular for elderly carers. Lise had resumed her paid work and carried this out in a way that enabled her to combine earning an income with looking after Eric. She had also become very active in a range of individual and collective advocacy initiatives and had developed skills and confidence in this capacity, which in some ways gave her a new lease of life.

Summary

Chapters 3 to 5 have told the individual stories of 12 current and former carers, and have highlighted the distinctiveness of the histories and experiences of care-giving in the context of different familial relationships and broader social, political, cultural and economic circumstances. These stories have been reconstructed in chronological order from narratives that were generated in the course of lengthy life-history interviews. The summaries at the end of each chapter have illustrated some of the ways in which a biographical perspective is valuable in understanding experiences of care-giving and responses to this, and in the 'key issues' following each story I have identified conceptual issues which will be developed throughout the book. In the next chapter I move on to consider what these stories have to say about the nature of care-giving and its relationship to an 'ethic of care' as well as to a sense of fairness and social justice.

CHAPTER 6

Carers' Perspectives on Care-Giving

The way in which these carers described their experiences of caring provides a valuable insight into the diverse ways in which this experience becomes part of their lives and what it meant to them. As well as reflecting on caring in the context of life histories, as I have done in the previous three chapters, we can also consider how carers talked about care-giving and to start to relate this to an ethic of care and to social justice. This will enable us to make links between the personal and social significance of care-giving.

The research reviewed in Chapter 1 illustrated the various ways in which caring and care-giving have been described, categorised and conceptualised. Much of that research involved talking to carers directly about their experiences, and so it is not surprising that a detailed analysis of what these 12 carers said about their experience would support previous conclusions about the emotional as well as physical and organisational labour involved in care-giving, the significance of what Nolan *et al.* (1996) have described as anticipatory care and as (re)constructive care, as well as the frustrations lay carers often experience in their relationships with statutory agencies. But here I am adopting a rather different perspective through which 'what is going on' within caring relationships can be understood in terms of ethics and rights. This is intended to counterbalance what can be an overly functional approach to caring and to introduce a discussion of the significance of care-giving beyond the specific interpersonal relationships of care-givers and care-receivers.

Talking about care-giving

There was plenty of talk about the tasks of care-giving in the interviews I carried out – whether they be physical tending, nursing care, dealing with financial, legal and household arrangements, or negotiating, co-ordinating and sometimes supervising help provided from elsewhere. But often this was as a result of direct questions from me – these were rarely the issues which carers focused on spontaneously in telling me their stories. The way in which carers spoke about care-giving demonstrates a number of characteristics which also appeared to be significant as far as they were concerned.

In a previous book I wrote: 'Families in which caring responsibilities are both more intense and more long lasting than the provision of parental care to children until they reach independence are becoming more "normal". "Ordinary life" often includes living with people with "special needs".' (Barnes, 1997a, p. 135) Since then, policy makers have recognised this – at least in terms of how widespread the experience of giving and receiving care is. The introduction to the National Strategy for Carers, published by the British government in 1999, noted that: 'One in eight people in Britain is now a carer – looking after someone who is ill, frail, disabled or unable to cope' (Department of Health, 1999, p. 11). But there is still a sense in which care-giving is treated as something that is unusual and it is certainly something about which professional 'experts' feel entitled to offer advice to those who are engaged in such relationships (see Ramsay *et al.*, 2001). Once carers had been identified as a 'category' of quasi service users, they became not only an object of social policy, but also subject to professional gaze and commentary.

One of the immediate things that struck me about the stories told by the carers I interviewed was the matter-of-fact way in which many of them spoke about care-giving and the taken-for-granted nature of their involvement in it. Many had been involved in a variety of caring relationships during the course of their lives; in some cases their stories told of care-giving by other family members, and included accounts of the way in which the person now identified as the 'recipient' of care had also been a care-giver. For example, Gina spoke a lot about her sister who looked after her disabled son; Daniel's wife Margaret had not only looked after her parents but had also helped Daniel to care for his first wife, whilst Emily's husband Edward had had responsibility for aspects of the care of his elderly aunts.

Bridget's discourse of caring is located within a cultural context in which it was taken for granted:

BRIDGET: …my father's brother lived with us at the beginning, and he died in our house and we nursed him, obviously. So it's in-bred in you from a young age in most farming communities back in the 40s, I was born in '41.

INTERVIEWER: So this is a farming community in Ireland.

BRIDGET: Yes, little village, very small village. So care in the community was already automatic, not just in our house, in every other house as well.

Whilst Lise accepted her care for her husband as part of what had been a life with many hardships:

Having had all the knocks before, also had with my mother who was only 61 when she died. You know, um [pause] I didn't think it was punishment or that I was hard done by. It was a hard life, it was extremely hard, but that's what life is about [pause] and it did not worry me.

Similar ways of talking can be found in other interviews. This acceptance that care-giving is part of what life is about reflects what Qureshi and Walker (1989) found in their study of family carers of older people and is further evidence of the enduring nature of the responsibilities kin feel for each other. That such responsibilities are gendered was also evident from these interviews, although as the example of Alan indicates, factors other than gender can determine who takes on caring roles.

What was also evident is how stories of care-giving were interwoven with other stories of family life, particularly in the case of Emily, Bridget and Gina. Emily talked a lot about her sons, their education, work and families, as well as about her own and her husband's siblings, aunts and uncles. She spoke about her own activities and interests – including the work in which she had been engaged for some years in documenting her family history. Bridget's story of looking after her mother was interwoven with the awful tale of a car accident that killed her nephew and seriously injured her brother. She spoke of the impact of this on other family members as well as her and her mother. Lise's life story reflected not only on the impact of public events, but on more personal crises. As well as telling the story of Irena's life and of their lives together once she became her carer, Gina talked of her sister's family, in particular her disabled nephew, and of her own children's education and jobs.

The impact of all this was to reinforce the sense of care-giving being one part of lives which include many other dimensions. This is rather less evidently the case for young parents of disabled children. Rose was at a stage where her anxiety about Surya and her current absorption in her care meant her story was more exclusively focused on this, but she too talked of her wish to resume her education, and of Arif's ambition to be a teacher.

One of the effects of research into carers' lives and of the campaigning of carers' organisations has been to emphasise the experience of caring not only as a problem and a burden, but also as something that is somehow distinct and separate from the rest of life. To give one example: Jones and Rupp (2000) describe the narrative approach to interviewing in the Cultures of Care project. They emphasise that it was the interviewee's frame of reference that they wanted to structure the interview, so carers were invited to speak about their experiences in response to the following opening:

> We're interested in the experiences of people caring for a family member, so I would like you to tell me about your experiences. I'm interested in how you came to take on the responsibility of caring, whether difficult decisions and choices had to be made and how the situation has developed and what kind of support or help you had? Also which aspects of caring are the most difficult ones for you? Which offers of assistance were made but rejected by you and how do you feel about being a carer and what it has meant for your life? (p. 277)

This opening, which was intended to enable the interviewee to determine the frame of reference, contains its own frame of reference which assumes care is 'difficult'. The authors note that the invitation to carers to tell their stories addressed many issues 'theoretically linked to care issues' and that there are other spheres of life that might dominate carers' constructions of their stories, but they make no acknowledgment of the potential impact of the bias contained within the opening gambit on the way in which carers were invited to speak.

One exception to this emphasis on caring as a problem has been the work of Nolan *et al.* (1996) which also identified the satisfactions of caring, but which still tends to isolate care-giving from other aspects of shared and individual lives over a life course. I am *not* arguing that care-giving is unproblematic, nor that there are not times when it dominates carers' lives and makes it difficult if not impossible to pursue other activities and interests. But what I am suggesting is that an emphasis on 'caring as problem' has a tendency either to pathologise, or treat as heroic, something that is actually part of the ordinary life of many people, interwoven with awareness of and concerns about other family members and friends, as well as the person to whom support is being provided; and which is often balanced with earning a living, following an education or pursuing other activities which provide a source of satisfaction and contribute to the health and well-being of the care-giver. Policies and practices that ignore the significance of these other engagements and isolate caring from other aspects of life are unlikely to be helpful either to carers or to the people they are supporting.

Mo Ray (2000) looked at the impact of chronic illness on long-term marriage relationships and identified the way in which both partners define and construct new roles and responsibilities associated with care in the context of those relationships. She writes: 'The narratives of both partners provide important insights into the ways in which, for example, marriage biographies or identities were used as a backdrop in the maintenance, or reconstruction, of identity when the transitions created by disability threatened long-standing continuities' (p. 166). It is possible to identify similar continuities in the way in which parental and filial carers spoke about care-giving. Nell, for example, spoke about the similarity in the nature of her concern for her son Derek and for her disabled son James. She talks about a 'mother's instinct' to protect her young and described how she reacted to news of Derek's redundancy by sending a cheque to him and his wife:

> And they both rang up and said there was no need for you to do that. But I said, but you haven't asked for anything and I want to let you know I am there for you. It's not like they are round the corner and I can pop them boxes of groceries in. So it's not just James: you will always protect, um, you know, I wanted to know that they were all right.

Susan felt guilty that she found it hard to enjoy spending time with her father after his injury had resulted in significant changes to his behaviour and personality. She talked about the way in which he no longer went out or took part in the activities he used to, but she also looked for ways in which she could identify aspects of how he used to be which were part of the close relationship she used to have with him:

> Um, but it was [pause] he still had that sociable quality about him, but without actually wanting to go anywhere. And I remember, um, coming home one day and I had met some guy and he was from XXXX. And I—we were going home to pick up my daughter and then we were going out. And I took him home and within, oh, thirty seconds of being through the door my dad got a bottle of whiskey out. 'You must stay,' er, he would say to my mum, 'Get this lad some food.'

When Alan took on responsibility for looking after his mother he found himself reflecting that this was not the first time in his life that he had looked after her, and he recognised a continuity in the nature of the relationship he had with her at different stages of his life. But, for him, caring for his mother was also an extension of his professional life. There were very practical expressions of this – members of the care team he put together had all worked for him when he worked for a social care agency. More subjectively he reflected on the importance of caring values defining both professional and lay care:

> I never believed from being an 18-year-old student nurse about the crap about controlled emotional involvement and professional distance. I never believed it because [pause] um, the reason that I did the jobs I did which was, you know, the caring jobs, still involved in that, but the actual direct care was because, you know, my values and my motives were that I had seen so much crap. You know, particularly my first job working in a large psychiatric hospital, seeing elderly blokes die in the middle of the night in all sorts of conditions. And I thought, people shouldn't—that shouldn't happen to people.

The varying ways in which carers looked for continuity in terms of their identities, relationships and in the identities of those they supported reinforced the sense of the importance of understanding caring as interwoven throughout their lives. Although some spoke of significant changes or transitions when a disabled child was born, a parent moved in, a husband or wife became chronically ill, their stories as a whole emphasised the way in which these carers constructed care-giving in the context of their whole lives, both in terms of the nature of the relationships in which they were involved and also the values which were important to them.

One characteristic of lay care relates to the particularity of the knowledge and understanding that family carers develop which enables them to provide 'person-centred' care based in intimate knowledge and shared histories (for example, Abrams, 1978). In the case of a severely disabled child who is unable to communicate verbally, the close and detailed knowledge which comes from the intense interactions they have with care-givers is vital to the assertion of their personhood. Rose's description of the way in which she and Arif understood how Surya responded to situations, what she did and did not enjoy and the way in which she is aware of and seeks to interact with others is a clear example of this. I have written about this elsewhere in relation to parents of children with learning diffi-culties who become frustrated and angry when the understanding and expertise they develop in communicating with daughters and sons unable to use verbal language is not recognised by others (Barnes, 1997b).

All the mothers' narratives demonstrated both the particular knowledge and the personally directed nature of lay caring relation-ships. Nell's accounts of James using his manipulative skills to get what he wanted, and how she had challenged him and not let him get away with this; Barbara's concern about the degree of William's capacity to 'make friends' with strangers; and Pauline's report of understanding Simon's language when others could not, are all examples of this. For both Nell and Pauline there had been times when they were on the receiving end of violent acts by their sons, which emerged out of the particularity of their relationships. Both women understood the frus-trations and hurt that gave rise to those acts because of their knowl-edge of their sons, but both were equally clear that it was important that they did not 'excuse' such actions, or similar actions directed at others, because they wanted their sons to be able to take part in social life and to understand how to build effective relationships. Nell talked about her reaction when it was suggested she should take James home from the hospital after he had set her house on fire:

And the hospital checked me over because of my heart, and said I could go. And then they said 'Oh you better take your son with you.' I said 'Where do you suggest I take him, I haven't got nowhere to bloody go myself.' So she said, 'Oooh well the social worker said you have got to take him.' I said, 'How amazing, how amazing.' Social workers tell me he has got all these rights. He can go and get drunk if he likes. He can go and visit prostitutes if he likes. But suddenly when he has got nowhere to go, he is my responsibility. And I said 'I am walking out of here and I don't care if you put him on XXXX Road and he is raped, murdered and mugged. I am going.' It broke my heart, it did. It really broke my heart to do it. And, um, I had to go and find accommodation for six weeks.

Carers who are sons and daughters also bring to the caring relationship a knowledge of their parents as they were when they did not need the level of support now provided by their offspring. These carers know what is important to their parents and what gives them pleasure: old films, in Alan's mother Catherine's case, or cooking, in Gina's mother Irena's case. Sons and daughters also have an insight into their parents' values and what is difficult as well as positive about their personalities. This knowledge is important both in sustaining quality of life and selfhood, including ensuring respect for their cultural values and the expression of these (for example, Bridget saying Hail Marys with her mother for long-dead relatives), but also in being able to challenge them when their behaviour becomes unacceptable either to their carers or to others. It enables them to ensure that the wishes of their parents are respected when they are not able to assert these themselves, as when Susan insisted on the type of funeral her father would have wanted.

Filial carers also develop new knowledge and understanding of their parents in this situation and they learn much about themselves. Gina learnt more about her mother's resourcefulness and the extent of reciprocity in their relationship. Both Alan and Bridget suggested that they achieved times of closeness with their mothers towards the end of their lives that they had not experienced when they were younger. Alan spoke of the way his mother developed contentment in his company and in her environment which contrasted with the much more troubled nature of their relationship when both were younger:

INTERVIEWER: What did you want for her?

ALAN: Well, to have dignity. To maybe come to terms with some things which I think she did a little bit...But maybe to be at peace. And, you know, [pause] in the last couple of years, particularly as the dementia really took hold, and she was, in a sense—I mean she used to shout and scream and various sorts of things, but there were other times when, yes, she would sit and watch the TV and she didn't have a glass in her hand, and she wasn't drunk. And she was laughing and she would go outside and, you know, look at the flowers and I would get her out of her wheelchair and sit her on a rug on the grass, which she wouldn't have been able to do. And that's ordinary, you know

Alan also said he had learnt how better to receive care himself, and was able to develop a closer relationship with his nieces and nephews as a result. Susan found herself challenged when she recognised the difficulty she had being with her father when her relationship with him was so different after his accident, but she was able to use what she had learnt in her work for a carers' organisation and spoke with pride about what she had achieved through this. All had engaged in processes of reflection about themselves and others.

There are many ways in which shared histories and the intimacies of marriage and other partner relationships can affect caring relationships (G. Parker, 1993). In the immediate aftermath of Eric's stroke Lise was the only one who could communicate with him because he reverted to German, which medical staff could not understand. Daniel stressed the importance of regular conversation for Margaret which he could provide because his attention was focused solely on her and he could bring to that conversation the experience of their lives together, even if she could not remember this. Emily was able to help Edward continue to engage in activities that he valued and they had enjoyed together for some time after his dementia meant that he was losing contact with his past.

As many of the interview extracts demonstrate, this intimate and personal knowledge was often connected with aspects of care-giving which were concerned very directly with ensuring that the rights of care recipients were respected. This happened in a number of contexts: in seeking to ensure that the help received from medical or social services were appropriate, responsive to personal and cultural circumstances and delivered in a timely manner; in maximising opportunities for safe and effective participation within their communities (see also M. Barnes, 1997a, ch. 8, and Traustadottir, 2000); and in ensuring that people's wishes about how they could live their lives were respected as much as possible. Carers were also aware of their own rights in these situations, although Nell's explicit use of the language of rights in talking about this was rather atypical. Although 'care' and 'rights' are often seen to exist in two distinct moral universes, the way in which carers spoke about care-giving suggests they did not recognise such a separation.

The five accounts of mothers of disabled children were rather different in the way in which notions of care and of rights appeared. All made some reference to having to assert their rights to receive help from statutory service providers, but in Pauline's account this was a theme running through the whole narrative, whilst in the case of Rose it appeared on only one occasion. Standing up for the rights of their disabled son or daughter was often linked with their intimate and particular knowledge of their child: Violet seeking to observe Gloria's treatment because she knew she was unhappy about it, Rose's sadness that her family were excluding Surya because of their lack of under-standing and fear. Nell was very clear that she expected James to be able to take part in the activities a young man might expect, but she also was assertive to ensure he was not exploited in the course of this:

> the one care assistant who used to take James to a brothel. But then I found out he wasn't only taking James he was taking this Asian man and James was paying for the three of them. And I am not opposed to James having sex, I'm really not, and if James needs to pay for sex and he can afford it, fine, but I don't see why he should pay for someone else.

A sense of 'unfairness' about the situation they found themselves in was something that these mothers felt at some points in their lives, but it was not pervasive. They were concerned that they got the best deal possible for their children, whilst also recognising their own needs for care and recognition.

In different ways and for different reasons, Alan, Susan, Bridget and Gina cared for their parents because they thought it was the right thing to do. Whilst a feeling of unfairness emerged for some of them from time to time – both in relation to their own position and that of the parent they supported – they did not question the rightness of what they were doing. This was in part a taken-for-granted aspect of what families are about, but there were more self-conscious aspects as well.

Alan had made a promise to his mother that she would not go into a nursing home. Both she and he knew that her personality and behaviour were such that this would be a difficult option. The time they had together towards the end of her life was used by Catherine to reconstruct her assessment of herself as a mother and Alan did not challenge this, even though it did not coincide with his or his siblings' experiences. An important aspect of the care he provided was to enable her to find some peace with herself, and he respected her right to reconstruct her life in a way that would ease her final years.

These carers used their knowledge and understanding of their parents to do what they could to ensure they received the type of help that would be acceptable to them and meet their needs. This was often not easy because they were not always given the information they needed to access help. But when they did have that information they used it, if necessary fighting for what both they and their parents were entitled to. Once Gina became involved in a carers' group she became much more aware of the financial and other help to which she and her mother were entitled. Because her sister also cared for her disabled son they were able to share information:

> I can fight for my mum and I have got access to knowledge. So that's fine. I can find things out, my sister is with [name of town] Carers. She is very involved. She organises walks for people…she is doing a lot. And she has got masses of literature and I find things out from her. So we pass things on to each other. But the worse thing of all is finance

There was a sense of injustice, in particular amongst older carers, that the promise held out by the welfare state was not being realised:

> I feel very annoyed over the conditions the country's treating people like me, if you like. I mean, there's not so many of us left, I suppose, now. From the Second World War, we must be getting a bit thin on the ground. People like me, we've worked all our working lives. We paid the taxes, we went in to the National Health Service when it was started, we've paid that, and we were promised everything would be there for us and that, when we wanted it. (Daniel)

The stories of the three partner carers also demonstrate the way in which intimate and particular knowledge is often very important in helping maintain personhood, sustain people's participation and inclusion in social life and get access to the support services and medical treatment that is needed. Daniel's story indicates that carers may also have to be alert to ensuring very basic needs are met by paid care providers. Like Bridget in the case of her mother, he found it necessary to ensure Margaret was getting sufficient to eat and drink whilst she was in residential care. Both Emily and Lise had to fight to get support services and Emily was angry that the failure to provide adequate support had put her life in danger. Whilst Daniel was immensely sad because of what was happening to Margaret he was also aware that both practical and emotional expressions of care and support were focused on her, and he was left with a sense that he himself only remained of value to ensure that she was looked after. It is very hard in these circumstances to distinguish their rights as carers, and the rights of the husbands and wives they were supporting. Both the concept and practice of care and rights are intimately bound up together.

An ethic of care

At this point I want to introduce the concept of an *ethic of care*, which provides a useful frame of reference not only for understanding the way in which the individual carers talked about care-giving and its place in their lives, but also for understanding care-giving in its social context – to address the significance of caring in the context of social relations and the way in which we live together. My discussion of an ethic of care draws primarily on the writings of Joan Tronto (1993) and Selma Sevenhuijsen (1998). Both writers are political theorists, which is not a discipline that is often considered immediately relevant to social care practitioners, but, as I hope to show, their perspectives offer a helpful way of thinking about what care-giving is and how social policies and practices might better support those involved in caring relationships. They both argue that caring should be understood in a political context as well as an interpersonal one. Here I focus primarily on the interpersonal dimension of an ethic of care and develop the political aspect of this argument in Chapter 8.

Both start from the centrality of care to all our lives. Tronto offers a definition which expands the concept of care from relationships between individuals to one which also encompasses the way we relate to ourselves and to our environment in order to 'maintain, continue and repair our "world" so that we can live in it as well as possible' (p.103). Whilst this means that the range of what we might understand as care is very broad, Tronto also argues that some activities and practices that are labelled 'caring' in fact do not fit this definition. For example, she distinguishes activities that constitute 'protection' from those characterised as caring, and suggests that 'caring work', for example, checking someone's vital signs in a nursing home, can be done without a caring disposition. She offers a familiar analysis of caring as consisting of: caring about, taking care of and care-giving, but draws an important distinction between 'taking care of' – which does not necessarily imply face-to-face, hands-on caring – and care-giving: for example, a social services manager may 'take care' of the needs of older service users in his patch by organising a team of social workers and allocating duties to them. She also adds to this 'care-receiving', in order to focus attention on the impact on and response of the person receiving care: 'It is important to include care-receiving as an element of the caring process because it provides the only way to know that caring needs have actually been met.' (p.108)

Tronto identifies four ethical elements of care:

1. *Attentiveness.* Without an awareness of and attentiveness to the needs of others it is not possible to act to meet those needs. One must both be able to 'suspend one's own goals, ambitions, plans of life, and concerns, in order to recognize and to be attentive to others' (p. 128), and be attentive to one's own needs for care to understand that the need for care is something that all of us experience, not something restricted to needy 'others'.

2. *Responsibility.* Attentiveness without action cannot constitute a caring morality. Thus taking responsibility for action is the second element of an ethic of care. Tronto notes that the concept of responsibility is usually conceived in relation to a requirement to conform to obligations, but she understands this as more of a sociological than a political or philosophical concept and argues that responsibility to act is embedded in a set of implicit cultural practices, rather than existing as a set of formal rules to be followed. Thus an ethic of care does not presuppose a particular type of action, and the notion of responsibility needs to be understood much more flexibly.

3. *Competence*. A concern with the impact of care implies that one
    dimension of an ethic of care must be that caring work should be
    competently performed. Tronto notes that in some large bureau-
    cracies 'taking care of' appears to be performed without any
    concern about the outcomes.
4. *Responsiveness*. Because caring takes place in situations where there
    are greater or lesser degrees of vulnerability: 'the moral concept
    of responsiveness requires that we remain alert to the possibilities
    of abuse that arise with vulnerability' (p. 135). For Tronto this
    means that we should consider the position of the care-receiver
    from their perspective. Responsiveness in turn requires attentive-
    ness, which demonstrates the need for all four elements to be inte-
    grated in order to develop knowledge and act in a thoughtful way
    in relation to the situations, needs and competences of other
    actors.

Both Tronto and Sevenhuijsen distinguish the significance of an
ethic of care to the moral order of society from an assumption that it
is 'naturally' women's responsibility to ensure that such a morality is
evident in practice. They also recognise that the achievement of social
relations characterised by an ethic of care is not just down to the
choices and actions of individuals in the way in which they relate to
each other, but that political structure and power relationships are
deeply implicated in this as well. Sevenhuijsen argues for a 'political
concept of an ethics of care which is able to embody insights from
feminist ethics' (1998, p. vi). She notes the distinction in the language
usually applied to a discussion of issues of citizenship and justice in the
public sphere from the vocabularies more usually applied to the
private world of care-giving: enforceable authority, rights and duties
usually define our notions of a citizenship made manifest in the public
sphere, whilst the private sphere of care-giving is discussed in terms of
the virtues of compassion, attentiveness, empathy and attention to
detail. One of the major achievements of feminist thinking has been
to 'blur the boundaries' between the public and the private sphere in
terms of both the way in which gendered power relationships structure
private lives as well as public policies, and in recognising the different
spaces and places in which women can exercise agency and express
their citizenship (Lister, 1997). One consequence of this is that it
becomes more possible to use the 'private' vocabulary of care-giving
to talk about social relations in the public sphere.

But issues of rights and care have often been argued to exist in different moral spaces, most evidently in this context by some within the disability movement who, in presenting disability as a civil rights issue, rejected the relevance of care as a basis on which to provide the kind of support to enable disabled people to live their lives as they want (for example, C. Barnes, 1991; Wood, 1991). During the first phase of modern feminism (from the end of the 1960s) the issue of care was seen in terms of the rights of women carers to reject an identity imposed upon them. Paradoxically, the language of rights was embraced by feminists writers on caring (for example, Finch and Groves, 1983) and this rights claim on the part of women carers was one source of conflict with the disability movement which was using the same language to assert the rights of those cast in the role of care recipients. Both Tronto and Sevenhuijsen are concerned to move beyond this binary opposition between justice (rights) and care. In charting her own history of working in this area, Sevenhuijsen recognises the importance of the early feminist work in focusing attention on the relationship between the family and the state, in naming care as labour and exposing the gendered assumptions behind what is paid and what unpaid labour. She discusses the significance of the work of Virginia Held, an American philosopher, who has criticised currents in moral philosophy which 'view moral problems solely as a conflict of rights between individuals' (Sevenhuijsen, 1998, p. 11). Taking as a model the relationship between mother and child, Held argues that to view moral dilemmas as conflicts between rights claims made on behalf of competing individuals is inadequate and incapable of recognising the significance of dependence and nurturing in human relationships: 'Instead of taking as its premises self-sufficient, atomistic individuals, ethics should start from processes of connection and individuation' (p. 12). But Sevenhuijsen argues that Held's conceptual framework could lead to the reproduction of 'moral motherhood' and that it is important to place such debates about moral philosophy within a political context.

Although both Tronto and Sevenhuijsen argue the morality of care, their aim is not to define such a morality in terms of a precise set of rules, nor to define 'carers' as a distinct group which alone has the responsibility for ensuring that social relations embody such a morality. In contrast, their work argues that 'carer' is not a fixed identity and 'caring' is not a universal set of practices. At different points in people's lives most of us will assume the roles both of care-giver and care-receiver and recognition of this is vital to overcoming the tendency to locate vulnerability in 'needy others' rather than ourselves. *Because* care and ethics are social practices and the moral dilemmas associated with caring are not made in the abstract but in the messiness of day to day circumstances and relationships, how people interpret the situations they are in, the way in which they construct meanings from those situations, and how both care-giver and care-receiver are able to exercise agency within those situations, are all important in determining precisely what care consists of. The motives which prompt care do not necessarily determine the quality of the care that is provided, and the social and institutional context within which it is provided as well as the nature of the relationship between the actors concerned will affect both what is possible and what might be considered 'good caring'.

Brechin *et al.* (2003) have demonstrated care-givers' own understanding of this through empirical research which involved groups of care-givers discussing vignettes designed to highlight what might be understood to be 'poor care'. What was evident from these discussions was that, whilst it was possible to identify specific themes around which care-givers constructed their responses to the situations with which they were presented, they were not judging the actions of care-givers in the vignettes by reference to some fixed set of criteria for 'good' and 'bad' care. Brechin *et al.* suggested that what they were in fact engaged in was a process of 'co-constructing an ethics of care' (p. 173) through a process of reflection and interpretation in which all aspects of the situation, including the history of the relationship as far as they knew it, were factors to be taken into account.

Ethics of care and lived lives

This perspective can also enable us to return to the accounts of the care-givers whose stories I have told in this book, in order to understand more about the way in which they were understanding and negotiating care as an ethical social practice. I have already discussed the way in which caring was accepted as part of ordinary life by these carers, and that their stories reveal that it is not only when people are engaged in the type of relationship recognised by policy makers and service providers as 'caring' that this is a significant aspect of their relationships with others. These stories also illustrate the extent to which the same people are likely to be both care-givers and care-receivers at different times during their lives, and sometimes at the same time. The ethics of care perspective enables us to highlight other aspects of their accounts that are significant in understanding the meaning of caring from their perspectives.

Firstly, there is the importance of caring for oneself as well as others. The experience of giving care to others had enabled carers to understand the importance of caring for one's self. Nell's inability to care adequately for herself after her husband's death led her into a new relationship which she subsequently recognised was a mistake from her point of view and which contributed to James's difficulty in dealing with his father's death and other things happening in his life at that time. Emily knew she needed to care for herself when she started to become ill, but was unable to get statutory agencies to act on this and provide her with the necessary support. The point in her interview where she showed most emotion was when she talked about her inability to enable Edward to die at home because the failure to care for her meant she had to be admitted to hospital. Barbara's own disability meant she was particularly aware of the need for care for herself (and of care-receivers' responses to care) and after William's birth this need was even more acute. Rose's decision to return to college to complete her education was one way of caring for herself, as was Susan's decision to keep Saturdays for herself. Daniel experienced an absence of care for himself and as a result saw his value in life as limited solely to caring for Margaret. Alan had learnt from his experience of looking after his mother how better to receive care from others.

For most of these carers the issue of 'motive' was not part of the discourse, with the exception of Pauline who had chosen to adopt a disabled son, and Alan who rejected love as a basis for his care for his mother and instead identified the source of his decision as a promise made to her grounded in his knowledge both of her and of the nature of what her experience of care in a nursing home would be. The latter derived both from his knowledge of her and of the institutional care system. It was not part of my purpose to evaluate the care being given and received in any of the situations I was exploring, but from what I could tell an absence of love did not indicate that the outcome of care suffered in this instance.

All of these carers had accepted the responsibility to give care in the context of particular relationships and broader social and cultural contexts which indicated to them that this was the right thing to do. In many cases this had led to the development of an identity as a carer (which I discuss in more detail in Chapter 7), but the way in which they spoke did not suggest that most were conscious of such an identity and such a relationship as distinct from being a mother, daughter, son, wife or husband. Whilst some, such as Bridget and Violet, were conscious of the cultural expectations about caring within the communities into which they had been born, they did not talk about this as a constraint on themselves. An awareness of the non-essential difference between care-givers and care-receivers, as well as of enduring interdependencies and the shifting degrees of neediness at different stages of people's lives was important in the way in which care-givers constructed their notions of what caring is about:

> it's interesting to reflect on it all. Um, I think it's had a major impact on my life, not just for work, but in my personal and social development as well. Um, it makes me worry because I'm going to be looking after my mother at some point – she is sixty-five now. Although you know she hasn't had any major health problems. But um, I am aware that I will be a carer in a different way I was with my father. But I shall be a carer for my mother at some point. Um, and then will Amy ever – my daughter – ever be a carer for me? (Susan)

The significance of the situated knowledge that all these carers demonstrated in providing care and support for their relatives evidence the attentiveness and responsiveness which Tronto identifies as dimensions of an ethics of care. As I have demonstrated in my discussion of this aspect of carers' stories, these are closely linked not only with an *awareness* of the perspective of the care-receiver, but also with action which is focused on maximising opportunities for care-receivers to continue to take part in activities that are important to them, and to receive respect and recognition from others.

These stories also confirm Tronto's observation that 'taking care of' and 'care-giving' are usefully distinguished. There were a number of examples which indicated that public organisations charged with 'taking care of' the needs of disabled and older people were not giving care in practice, in the way in which they fulfilled their responsibilities. For example, one theme in a number of interviews was the delay in obtaining home adaptations necessary to enable disabled people to continue to live at home, and the unhelpful way in which such services were provided. More generally, the apparent unwillingness to be pro-active in giving information about services, benefits and supports available to care-givers and care-receivers can be understood as another example of 'taking care of' without 'giving care'.

Finally, we can identify examples in these stories where care-givers are engaged in the type of messy moral dilemmas that Sevenhuijsen suggests are typical of an understanding of ethics as situated rather than abstract and universal. Was Nell right to leave James at the hospital after he had set fire to her house? Should Pauline have sought to prosecute Simon after he broke in to her house and stole money? Should Daniel have objected to the fact that Margaret was put in a chair from which she could not move unaided in the nursing home? These types of very real dilemmas that carers face, which concern not only their own actions, but how they should respond to the actions of others, have to be resolved in the context of the nature of the relationship in which they are involved, the history of that relationship, their own needs and circumstances, as well as those of the care- receiver. An important part of what caring means is confronting such dilemmas and working out what to do within the particular context in which care is being given and received. It is not about learning and applying the rules, even though the carers themselves are likely to find themselves confronted by normative expectations of how families *should* behave in different situations (see Gubrium and Holstein, 1990, p. 60).

Summary

In this chapter I have explored what care-giving meant to the twelve carers whose stories I told in Chapters 3 to 5. Rather than seeking to analyse carers' accounts by reference to categories of care I have interpreted their stories as a whole and looked at how carers spoke about the particular caring relationships which were the focus of the interview in relation to other aspects of their lives. I have emphasised what can be considered the *ordinariness* of care-giving as well as the way in which particular experiences are informed both by cultural and personal backgrounds. I have outlined feminist concepts of an ethics of care and used this to develop an understanding of what care-giving means in the context of real life relationships. This approach to care-giving emphasises the need to understand caring in a political as well as personal context and it is to this that I turn in the next two chapters.

CHAPTER 7

Carers and the Carers' Movement

Most of the carers whose stories I have told in this book had publicly identified themselves as carers by becoming involved in carers' groups. Some were involved in individual and collective advocacy on behalf of carers. In this chapter I discuss what contribution the carers' movement has made to understanding the nature of caring relationships and to the broader significance of care as a social good. I also consider the impact of the carers' movement in the context of other user movements on social work and social care policy and practice. First let us look at the way in which these carers talked about their more public identities as care-givers and what this meant to them. In discussing these personal experiences I also suggest how these experiences relate to other aspects of the stories they recounted of their lives before and after becoming carers.

Personal experiences

For Pauline – in the context of an account in which battling with and challenging professional service providers featured as a significant dimension of her narrative – her first experience of meeting with other parents of disabled children was significant: 'It felt as though we were part of a community.' She spoke of feeling apart from other parents: 'I sometimes think you couldn't tell anybody, neighbours or anybody that I know, the experience of handicapped 'cause they just wouldn't understand. And I don't even try.' So when she met up with others who did understand such experiences this was a great relief. She said of a woman she met visiting her son in the special unit to which he was admitted that they were able to 'blow their top' with each other. And when she met parents of sons or daughters with mental health problems through Rethink (previously the National Schizophrenia Fellowship) she had an experience which she had not had in contact with other carers: 'And we have weekly meetings and you actually feel, it's like being in a foreign country and nobody understands the lingo you speak. Then all of a sudden you come back home and everybody understands.' Through Rethink she also started to receive advocacy support in her dealings with the unit to which Simon was admitted and recognised Simon's problems as mental health problems as well as those relating to learning difficulties. She first got involved with generic carers' groups when Simon was eight – these were collective advocacy groups. But she did not talk much about this and by the time of the interview was starting to distance herself from this – she felt there were other, more enjoyable things that she could spend her time on.

Rose spoke briefly about her involvement in carers' groups as a source of knowledge and ideas about what might be possible, learning from others who had experiences relevant to her own. It had become important for her to learn and to develop her own skills to support her daughter better. In her account she distinguished the responses of professional care-givers with those of lay carers who are emotionally involved and who have the particular knowledge from which professional care-givers can benefit. She valued the insights of others, like her, who were personally and emotionally affected by care-giving. Apart from needing to be assertive with doctors to ensure Surya would not be left to die if she became very ill, she had also experienced lack of understanding and support from other members of her family. There was evidence of an emergent sense of injustice in the way in which she spoke about her education having been cut short by her father. She had also learnt about her own problem – dyslexia – and how that had impeded her own development. In this context her regular contact with carers' groups gave her support to assert her own needs and perspectives. She had also become very aware of the impact of care-giving on others in a similar situation: she spoke of a friend who had a son who was autistic and had cerebral palsy and who looked after him 24 hours a day with little support from her husband.

Barbara's experience of care-giving started at school when she provided support to other disabled children. Later she cared for her mother, her father and then her son. She also worked in this capacity in children's homes. So she had a strong sense of herself as a carer.

Her narrative did not include accounts of having had to battle with statutory agencies, although she was anticipating the possibility of this. She also talked passionately about the importance of support being provided, for carers to receive respite, and for carers to be listened to and their knowledge respected. She was also aware that carers need knowledge of the system and their rights within it if they are to be able to assert their rights. Through her own experience of disability and her mother's experience of caring for her she was also aware of the importance of what carers can do to prevent disabled people from being seen as 'different' and how important it is that carers receive information to secure necessary support. In this context she talked about being involved in a number of different carers' groups and in a 'People's Panel' which is consulted on policy issues. This was important to her as a means of ensuring she was engaged in 'public' activities. But she didn't enlarge on her experiences of such involvement.

The experience of care-giving had shaped Nell's adult life and had a significant impact on her identity. She spoke of the way in which caring for James had undermined her sense of self-worth as well as being the source of an opportunity to develop considerable strengths. She had difficult early experiences with professional carers who were uncertain what was wrong with James and insensitive in the way in which they responded to her about his likely prognosis. She felt she had spent much of her time fighting the system and had achieved a lot from that: 'I can see, being my age and being a carer for the last thirty-six years, how things have changed. And if it wasn't for people like myself fighting the system, we would still be very much frowned upon as idiots and just a mother.' Her involvement with a carers' unit enabled her to 'keep my brain ticking over' and to keep in touch with developments in relation to community care. This had been particularly important for her since she stopped working after her heart attack.

Nell spoke of how caring had isolated her from friends and contemporaries because caring responsibilities did not reduce as James got older. But she also said she and her husband did not want to socialise only with other families with disabled children. Her account included a number of references to points at which she asserted her own rights as well as advocated for James's rights, including her encouragement to him to lead his own life. Talking about her involvement with carers' groups she said:

It hasn't all been hell. I mean I have met some lovely people. Some very nice people. And I mean in spite of my disability, with a heart problem, I've been able to continue with the carers' groups. And found out things and done things and I have felt I could talk to anyone. I can talk from the top to the bottom of the tree. That doesn't make any difference. Whereas I wasn't very high educated and I would have probably spent my working life in a factory or something. So I suppose in a way it's helped me to develop in that way. Although it sounds as if I'm blowing my own trumpet, I know how to get round the system. And I know how to help other people get round the system. Which gives me a great sense of achievement.

She went on to describe how she had got money from a bank to take a group of carers out for the day and how she had subsequently introduced a day centre manager to the bank to help her get support from them for equipment. She also said that James knew his mum was in a carers' group and was proud of what she did.

Alan's approach to care-giving was based in his professional experience which was itself informed by a value base which does not distinguish between a personal and a professional morality. His life story was presented as a coherent whole – his care for his mother took place when he was a child as well as in middle age and his paid work was in a variety of caring roles. He married a woman who also worked in this field. But this may also mean that he felt no need to become involved in carers' groups and he had taken a decision not to, as a matter of course, identify himself as a carer in the context of his professional work. The 'action' in which he was engaged was that in which he was engaged in his professional life. None of this means that he did not experience difficulties in his negotiations with professional care-givers, nor that he felt his own needs were adequately recognised by professionals, but his response was to use this in the way he advised and worked with professionals rather than through challenging service providers through action in a carers' groups. Here he talks explicitly about how his experience had influenced his professional practice:

I always used to think, what happens to people who don't know? You know what sort of deal carers get. And I knew that before, because of working with carers and everything else. But of course it's never the same until you actually do it and then once you actually do it and you get in my position where [pause] even now I go to meetings

where I still have to say, don't say users and carers, they are two
different groups. And don't say oh, what have we forgotten, we have
forgotten carers. You know I am still doing that now – and that's not
about resentfulness either. I suppose it is about being able to carry
that banner. But not necessarily say, you don't have to say all the
time I am a carer, or I was a carer: I don't. People who knew me at
the time, that was different. Do you know what I mean, people
know that I was at the time. But I don't do it now. I don't have to
say, well, you know this stems from personal experience. If I say it
it's got an authority. And some people recognise it straight away,
others don't.

Nevertheless he also acknowledged that there is a certain amount of
status attached to having been a carer when you also work 'in the business'.

The starting point for Gina's account was the hard times her
mother and the rest of the family had during the war. Her narrative
contains an awareness of persecution, of transitions, of being on the
outside and the disadvantage that can bring. Running through her
account are narratives of her mother's poor health and of financial
stringency. She became pro-active on her mother's behalf when she
took over her care from her father, and talked in some detail about the
battles she had to get the financial support and help with aids and
adaptations to which they were entitled. She became aware of the way
in which lack of information and knowledge gets in the way of access
to necessary support.

When I invited her to tell me more about herself, Gina did not
dwell on her own family but instead talked about the work she had
done for a social services user group. She had become the secretary of
that group and spent many hours working as a volunteer in the users'
and carers' centre. She had started to find that too hard in addition to
the support she was providing to her mother and to her sister and her
disabled son. She spoke of her motivation in doing this:

And I started doing, in the meantime the voluntary work to give
back some of the—because I felt obliged, you know if you get
something, you can't just say, oh well I am entitled to that. Yes I am
entitled to it, but you have to give something back if you can. So I
went to the [users group]. I help with the carers' group.

She used her skills to get carers involved in craftwork and she also insti-
gated outings. She reduced her involvement in the users' group
because of one man whose behaviour was 'trouble'. She described
herself as someone who could not say no when people ask her to do
something, but during the past year her own health had been deteriorating so she was having to learn. Her descriptions of her activity in
this context focused on a support and social role (secretary, crafts,
keeping the office in order, posting mail out), rather than one in which
she was actively campaigning. Although she had also worked on a
carers' 'surgery' for a while and she talked with pride about being
involved in a campaign to get free TV licences for disabled people. She
said: 'It's very important for us because we are a watchdog for all the
aspects of disability. And for the carers as well.' As well as feeling she
needed to put something back, she also described her involvement as
meeting a need to get out and about. She emphasised the importance
of this in relation to getting current information and making sure this
was passed on to people who needed it: she recognised there were
people who were in the situation she had been and she could help
them. She took information leaflets to leave in various public places,
and having identified herself as a 'carer' was now encouraging others
to do so: 'People don't know they're carers'. She spoke of the potential
effects of people not knowing the support to which they are entitled.
'It's the people who don't know, people who die in poverty. A 41-year-
old man who dies because he didn't know he could have a district
nurse come to see to the ulcer on his legs. He had an infection and
died.' She wanted to prevent people 'suffering in silence'.

Susan's experience of caring for her father led directly to her taking
a job with a carers' organisation. Her story narrates an experience of
care-giving with no information or support from statutory agencies
and thus caring as an isolated experience:

> We didn't know that there were areas to be accessed. We didn't
> know there were supports for carers. Um, we knew that there was
> support for Dad if we needed a doctor or whatever. But we didn't
> know that there was a carer support group. We didn't know that we
> could get people coming to sit with Dad while we went out. We
> didn't know we could actually send Dad somewhere for a weekend
> while we had some rest. Um, we just didn't know those things
> existed.

In retrospect she was able to be angry about that: 'especially with the job I am doing now I can see how outrageous the whole situation was. But at the time it was um, well, that's what we have to do. Doctors have said we will have to do that, and okay, we just get on with it.' She learnt from her own experience what is important to carers – in particular the need for a break which she ensured for herself by keeping one day a week for her own studying. She also recognised the differences between what she needed and what her mother would have benefited from in this situation:

> the isolation for mum has been and is now the worst thing ever. The fact that she never saw anybody apart from me and her grand-daughter…the thought of a carers' group, if Dad could have been left for a while, or if I'd been there, to have gone and spoken. I mean my mother can talk for England. So to have gone and spoken to other people who [pause] knew what it was like. Because as far as mum was concerned she was the only person in the world experiencing this…I was slightly different in that I didn't—I didn't know about the carer support group so I couldn't, I didn't go to them either. But by that time, um, I completely lost it and had to have three months off work with stress. Um, [pause] so I was at home and I was referred to a psychologist, a counsellor, rather, who I could at least talk things through with there.

She saw an advert for an advocacy project manager for carers and decided to apply because 'I would like to work for an organisation so that other people don't have to go through what we went through.' She described it as a gamble because it was a new job in a voluntary organisation and she had been used to the security of working for a local authority. She also had had a rather stereotypical view of the voluntary sector: 'I thought it's all twin set and pearls, they are not serious about it, there's no money in it, it's just people playing at work.' Her work with this organisation taught her more about carers – she commented on the difference between being born with a particular condition and being a carer all your life, and suddenly becoming a carer through accident or illness. She thought the latter was hard because 'you have known a different life'. She tried to get information packs into hospitals, GP surgeries and everywhere carers might be able to access these. She suggested that the psychological impact of her own experience – the guilt she felt and the emotionality of the experience – is what makes her good at her job, although she also had a sense that there is an expectation of emotional distance.

Susan was proud of a carers' befriending service that she had developed. This was based on her knowledge of her mum's isolation and what a difference it would have made to her to have someone coming to chat with her for a couple of hours. She suggested that it was hard to talk to people who don't have a similar experience because 'they don't want to keep hearing about how doom and gloom life is and how sad and depressed you feel all the time'. Hence there is a need for spaces where those for whom such experiences are a central part of life can talk with each other. She noted the public significance of this as: 'Until you become a carer yourself, you are not interested. I was never interested in carers before, until you become one you have no interest whatever.' Hence it is hard to promote carers' issues within the public sphere and it is necessary for those who have been carers to do this, and to suggest to others that they should be interested because they too may become carers. Susan ended the interview by talking about the growth in the organisation for which she worked – they were increasing their staffing and services, but still did not have enough for the services and support that they wanted to provide.

After Edward's death Emily continued to take an active interest in health and social care services. She also had an interest in ageing and older people, pursued in part through her involvement in the University of the Third Age. Education had been important to her and her family all her life. She talked at various points in the interview about the details of financial issues relating to ageing – both the need to move to a less expensive part of the country when Edward retired and the rules and regulations regarding payments for services in the light of the financial situation of recipients and their spouses. She was knowledgeable and sometimes cross about this, but somewhat reluctant to describe it as 'unfair'.

Her story also indicated a broader awareness and concern about policies, politics and changing lifestyles: she was committed to the use of public transport and angered by the solitary use of cars without any preparedness to share and offer lifts. In general her interview indicated a woman with a wide range of public and private interests. Her personal anger in relation to her own experience was primarily about the absence of concern for her health which led to serious illness, and to her husband having to be admitted to a nursing home where he died. When she was given information about a carers' association she decided to go and continued to attend these meetings although she was not always very impressed by them. She continued to attend because she felt she was the 'only representative of somebody who has really done 24 hours'. She thought the groups mainly comprised parents of disabled children rather than people who were or had been caring for a partner. She expressed dissatisfaction that health and social care agencies were spending too much time and money on producing reports and re-organising, rather than focusing on front-line services. She drew on her own experiences to comment about both delays in receiving services and failures to fully assess needs and prioritise services as a result. She knew other people in a similar situation who were getting no support.

Lise was an active member of a carers' group, of a social services users' group and of an older people's group. Central to her story is the experience of having come from a privileged background and then experiencing persecution and dislocation. Her religious and cultural background is key to her sense of identity. Her personal history was of a marriage in which her husband had held most of the power, but in which she had been assertive at key points, and after his stroke the balance of power shifted substantially, including Lise taking over responsibility for their financial affairs. She had to be assertive to ensure she got the resources and support she needed to look after him. No one provided her with any information so she had to search this out. She said she learned to be a rebel, turning to her MP for help when she did not receive what she thought she was entitled to. Talking about her need to use threats to ensure she got sufficient incontinence pads she said: 'I mean those were everyday happenings. Those were all – and once he was gone I thought, well if I can help somebody else not to have that struggle, and make them the way I was, stand on their own feet and not being talked down to'. Once she had made contact with carers' groups she strongly identified herself as a carer. She referred to the fact that she always spoke up when she had the opportunity because of the constant struggle she had to get what she and Eric needed. This was the first time she had been involved in any collective action or 'social affairs'.

Lise also talked about the way in which she encouraged friends and neighbours to assert their own needs. She gave the example of an elderly neighbour who had had a spinal operation and whom she encouraged to resist being sent home from hospital before the house was adapted so that he could go upstairs. She used this, as well as examples from her own experiences in deliberations with the Director of Social Services, to argue for increased resources being invested in occupational therapy and aids and adaptations. When I asked her whether she had changed personally as a result of her experience of caring for her husband she said: 'Yes I have become an expert. I was a very weak person before. But I learned to battle and I battle on.' She was starting to want to reduce the amount of work she did for the various groups in which she was involved because of her own age (79 at the time of interview), but she continued to take part four years later.

The carers' movement

The carers' movement in the UK grew from the awareness of unmarried women who had given up work to look after elderly parents that this was an unrecognised contribution to well-being and one that left them both isolated and financially disadvantaged. The first organisation to represent those who subsequently became known as carers was established in 1963 as the 'National Council for the Single Woman and her Dependant' (NCSWD). As this organisation grew and became more successful, married women looking after elderly parents also identified themselves with many of the experiences and issues raised by NCSWD and later those involved in other types of caring relationships also started to identify themselves with much of what was being said and with the campaigns that were being pursued. In 1988 the Carers National Association brought together carers in different circumstances in the first national organisation for all carers. Local groups and local projects started to burgeon, including both self-help and individual and collective advocacy, as well as initiatives taken by service providers to both consult with and offer support to carers (for more details of this history see M. Barnes, 1997a, ch. 5, and M. Barnes, 2001). Similar developments have taken place in Ireland (Collins-Hughes, 2001) where the Carers Association of Ireland was established in 1987.

The carers' movement is one part of a broader user movement which has challenged not only issues of service delivery and design, but more fundamental questions of the way in which we understand what it is to be old, disabled, mentally ill – or to provide and receive care. There are a number of aspects to this, many of which are evident in the way in which these carers spoke about their contact with and involvement in action over and above the direct provision of care-giving. Most fundamental is the issue of making visible experiences that, although they are increasingly common, are still insufficiently recognised and acknowledged as a significant aspect of what it is to be human. One of the effects of social policies which have, in the past, sought to separate disabled people, those with mental health problems and those who become frail in old age, from the rest of the population, has been that many people grow up never having social contact with older or disabled people and so both fear ageing and disability and do not understand it as an ordinary part of life. Those who live with and provide support to people in this situation feel themselves isolated from 'others' and are reluctant to talk about their lives and experiences because of the lack of understanding they receive and also because they are reluctant to 'burden' others with what this entails. Policies are made and social life goes on without sufficient acknowledgement of how these may exclude both older and disabled people and those who care for them. Frailty and increasing dependence on others is seen almost entirely in negative terms. This in turn contributes to the devaluing of those whose skills and work – paid and unpaid – are focused on meeting needs associated with physical frailty and/or mental confusion (Harrington Meyer, 2000).

The emergence of the carers' movement can be considered to have created the identity of 'carer' as a social group. This does not mean that the activity and experience of care-giving was invented by the movement, but the naming of carers as a social group in the UK enabled that experience to be formally recognised within official policy and in legislation – thus, carers have a legal right to an assessment of their needs and the New Labour Government launched a Carers' Strategy intended to value and support the work of care-givers. Much of the early emphasis of the carers' movement was on encouraging those who provided support to frail, ill or disabled family members and friends to identify themselves as 'carers'. As Gina noted, many who are in that position still do not do so and there are some who actively resist such an identity because they locate the support they provide in the context of another type of relationship: that of wife, mother, lover, for example. Similarly, many of those who receive help from a family member are reluctant to identify that person as a carer, rather than as, say, a husband, wife or partner (Henderson and Forbat, 2002).

This highlights one of the dilemmas which I am grappling with in this book: how to recognise the significance of those relationships which have come to be known by the term 'caring relationships', at the same time as understanding how those relationships are embedded within and embody relationships more usually framed in other terms. The imperative to understand this dilemma derives from the fact that care-givers and care-receivers themselves are engaged constantly in a process of negotiating this within their daily lives. It is a particular dilemma for younger spouses and partners when one partner becomes ill or disabled after the relationship has been established (see G. Parker, 1993), not least because of the challenge care-giving offers to the usual hopes and expectations which surround the start of such relationships. But difficult renegotiations are not exclusive to partner relationships. Susan's story, for example, demonstrated how difficult adult children can find it to re-negotiate their relationship with a parent in the context of radically changed circumstances, in this instance resulting from an unexpected accident.

The issue of identity is important in understanding the development of collective action. Melucci has suggested that a shared identity 'constructed and negotiated through a repeated process of "activation" of social relationships connecting the actors' (1985) is a key characteristic of what he termed new social movements. Thus, while some initial recognition of shared experience is necessary for the first phase of organisation, the process of identity construction is an on-going aspect of social movement organisation and action. This does not imply uniformity of identity, nor that an end point can be reached at which a collective identity becomes 'fixed'. In the early days of the disability movement, differences of identity within the movement (for example, relating to gender and ethnicity) were downplayed in the interests of establishing the shared experience of disablement resulting from the way in which society is organised on assumptions of able-bodiedness. As the movement developed, it has become more possible to acknowledge differences amongst disabled people and the particular oppressions associated with such differences – for example, the importance of beautiful bodies amongst gay men can make life particularly hard for disabled gay men.

The carers' movement started out with one group of care-givers identifying their distinct experience: unmarried women caring for elderly parents. That expanded so that a much broader organisation was developed to encompass what were seen as the shared interests and experiences of carers in different circumstances. For individuals who find themselves in what, for them, can be a new and unfamiliar situation that isolates them from both family and friends, and which faces them with challenges both in their relationships with each other and with service providers, making contact with others facing similar challenges can be both an affirmation and a relief. Gubrium and Holstein (1990) discuss the way in which support groups of carers of people with Alzheimer's in the USA create spaces in which new 'interpretive resources' (p. 64) can be developed which enable members to reconstruct what 'family' means in such situations. One aspect of this is in facilitating the exploration of definitions of responsibility in the context of the particular circumstances faced by family members caring for a relative with dementia (see Chapter 6).

Taking part in broadly based action which achieves official recognition and enables the experience and knowledge gained through caregiving to be applied in advocating and campaigning offers not only a boost to individuals' own sense of self-worth, but creates a sense that more widespread change is possible. It contributes to a process through which people both understand themselves as 'carers' and contribute to a broader conception and understanding of what 'being a carer' means, for those directly involved in caring relationships, for policy makers and service providers directly concerned with caring issues, and for others who may find themselves involved in such a relationship in the future. Alongside the broadly based groups and organisations there have always been support and advocacy groups based around the experiences of people in particular circumstances. Pauline's response to identifying a group that spoke her language is one indication of how important this can be in reducing the isolation felt by many care-givers.

The general point is that user and carer movements have provided spaces within which identities can be articulated separate from the construction of such identities by welfare professionals. Separate organisation has made that possible and continued action enables the process to develop, not only for existing members of the movement, but also for those who join at a later stage of its development. However, the importance of collective action amongst carers is not solely to achieve recognition for the role they play and the knowledge and skills they develop in so doing or, in the case of disabled people and users/survivors, to break free from demeaning or stigmatising identities deriving from stereotypical assumptions of incompetence or irrationality, or from medicalised constructions of pathological malfunctioning bodies or minds. What the social models of disability and ageing, the less well formulated but emergent thinking around social models of mental illness, and the usually un-theorised but powerful experiential knowledge of care-givers, offer are understandings of the way in which notions of madness and sanity, disabled and 'normal' bodies, youth and age, construct social relations within society. The particular significance of carers' perspectives on this is to focus our attention on the way in which it is not only individual disabled or frail older people who can find themselves disadvantaged and excluded in a society in which autonomy and independence are valued and dependence is regarded as a moral weakness.

In his later work Melucci reinforced his emphasis on the cultural significance of new social movements. He wrote: 'Contemporary "movements" assume the form of solidarity networks entrusted with potent cultural meanings, and it is precisely these meanings that distinguish them so sharply from political actors and formal organizations next to them' (Melucci, 1996, p. 4). Such movements are concerned less with the distribution of resources within society, and more with a transformation of meanings and values – in this context, with a transformation in the way in which we think about what it is to be old, to be disabled, to provide and receive care, to experience the confusing and sometimes frightening impact of psychological distress, and not only how we organise and provide welfare services to support those with need of support, but also how such experiences define and construct social relations in everyday life.

Symbolic and cultural objectives concerned with social relations, as well as the design of welfare services, require action within diverse locations – in the interactions of daily life; in the production of media and artistic representations; as well as in interactions between individual service users and welfare professionals, and in deliberation about the design of policy and service delivery amongst politicians and service providers. Carers' groups and organisations have given attention to the whole lives of care-givers, not just to helping them in their battles with welfare professionals. Thus it is not uncommon for carers' groups to organise social events, craft sessions, keep-fit classes or aromatherapy. Such groups aim to help carers care for themselves as well as for each other and the person to whom they provide support. They value and model caring as a moral basis for social relations.

Of particular significance in the context of understanding the way in which user and carer movements can challenge professionalised welfare systems is action in the context of knowledge production and

dissemination. Seidman has described this particular aspect of new
social movements: 'These new social movements created new subjects
of knowledge (African Americans, women, lesbians and gay men) and
new knowledges...Black nationalists, feminists, gay liberationists and
lesbian feminists produced social perspectives that were said to express
their distinctive social reality: Afrocentrism, feminism, lesbian and gay
or Queer theory' (Seidman, 1998, p.254). In addition to articulating
their own identities, service users, disabled people and carers can also
be seen to have produced new 'subjects of knowledge', evidenced, for
example, in the burgeoning of research into carers and caring following on from the articulation of the identity of carer. There could be no
research agenda about carers without the naming of carer as a category. And as the carers' movement has gained strength it, like other
user movements, has not simply influenced the way in which the issues
of ageing, disability and mental distress are conceptualised and
researched by others, but has also started to become involved in knowledge production through designing and undertaking its own research.
Gubrium and Holstein (1990, ch. 6) also note the way in which carers'
support groups assert a form of 'antiprofessionalism' by asserting the
significance of what they refer to as the 'privileged knowledge' of
insiders.

In these ways the carers' movement, together with other user movements, makes a significant contribution to the pursuit of social justice
– both in terms of the social rights of citizens to receive services which
can enable them to meet their basic needs and to practise their citizenship, but also in terms of rights to voice, to be part of the process
through which decisions are made that will affect their lives. My
perspective on social justice here draws from political theorists such as
Young (1990, 2000) and Fraser (1997) who argue that redistributive
notions of justice are inadequate in the context of diverse societies in
which forms of oppression are cultural as well as material, and that
opportunities for recognition and voice are essential 'for the development and exercise of individual capacities and collective communication and cooperation' (Young, 1990, p.39). The experience of
oppression can be as much about being denied the opportunity to have
a say about and exercise any influence over decisions which substantially affect the way in which you live your life, as it can be about more
direct experiences of domination by others. Those carers who become
active in the movement are usually motivated by their own experiences
of being unheard and unable to influence decisions about services and

support that affect themselves and those they care for. They take part in the hope that this will be a means through which they can become more influential for their own benefit, but, as these accounts show, they are also seeking to use their experiences to benefit others and may continue to be active in this way after their own experience of care-giving has come to an end, as in the case of Lise, or start their broader involvement at this point as Susan did.

Summary

Care-giving can be an isolating experience and developing contacts with other carers is a means of receiving support and recognition, and a basis from which to campaign for broader recognition of both care-givers and care-receivers. In this way the carers' movement can be considered to contribute to broader social justice objectives. An important characteristic of the carers' movement is that it has contributed to the development of a collective identity amongst carers, but this can also contribute to an identification of care-givers and care-receivers as distinct groups: it has tended to 'fix' such identities as separate rather than promote an understanding of the fluidity of care-giving and care-receiving during the life course.

CHAPTER 8

Achieving Social Justice Through Care

Introduction

In previous chapters I have focused on the private lives of care-givers and on the way in which some of those who identify themselves in this way take on public roles in the context of carers' groups and organisations. I have illustrated the way in which notions of care and justice are intertwined in the accounts of care-givers, and I have discussed this by reference to feminist theorisations of an 'ethic of care'. At a collective level, my discussion of the carers' movement has started to show how carers are pursuing justice for carers through achieving recognition and voice. I have suggested that, in making such a contribution to social justice, the carers' movement needs to be understood as part of a broader social movement, constituted of service users, disabled people, older people and others who are challenging the construction of those who use health and social care services as needy, dependent and lacking in agency.

But it is also important to consider the significance of care beyond the one-to-one relationships between those who at different points in their lives may be care-givers and care-receivers, and beyond the collective impact that the carers' movement is having in achieving recognition and justice for carers. Caring can also be important work for communities, strengthening them, enabling those least powerful to receive support and recognition, acting to resist oppression from outside and within. Care can fulfil a number of functions, including sustaining the connection between individuals at risk of exclusion and the communities within which they live, and asserting the humanity and value of people who may be devalued by society. This is important 'work' for society, even if those directly involved in caring relationships may not construct this in such a way. And it is also work that is undertaken by many people who would not be designated 'carers' in the context of social care policy and service provision. It is evident, for example, in the way activists in poor communities support people to find out about and access benefits and services to which they are entitled, and in the way mental health service users advocate individually and collectively for fellow users who are stigmatised and disempowered as a result of their mental distress.

There is a tension between recognising the value care contributes to community strength and cohesion, and constructing it as a normative responsibility of active citizenship. Perhaps the key issue here is: on whose terms is care being negotiated and provided? In this context, the collective voice of carers as one group of voices amongst others giving expression to the experiences of people in danger of being excluded or marginalised is important not only as a means of influencing state welfare, but also to argue for social relations based in an ethic of care as well as justice.

My argument here is that a proper valuing of care as an essential aspect of social relations has benefits not only for care-providers and care-receivers, but also for general social well-being. We need to rescue the concept and practice of care both from the impact of those who regard it as something that is carried out as a natural part of women's natures as wives, mothers and daughters, and thus not a matter for public regard, or as a menial task that can be allocated to those in no position to demand a decent wage, as well as from those who equate care with practices that are controlling, smothering and disempowering. To do so requires policies and practices based in a wholehearted acceptance of an ethic of care, alongside a commitment to social justice that includes care-givers and care-receivers, and recognises that the same person can be both, at the same and at different times.

We also need to think about social relations and the values underpinning these in the context of changing population structures in developed and in developing societies, changing concepts and practices of family life, the social as well as personal challenges resulting from chronic health problems, and the disruptive impact of civil war and international conflict. Not only do we need a concept and practice of social justice which can respond to populations in which there is an increasing percentage of old and very old people, and in which more people are living longer with long-term health problems, we also need a concept and practice of justice which responds to the circumstances of those who have been traumatised by conflict and who have had to uproot themselves and their families to seek safety in another country. A notion of justice limited to liberal notions of 'rights' is inadequate to respond to such circumstances.

In this chapter I draw out the broader implications of understanding care as contributing to an inclusive concept and practice of social justice. I address contemporary discourses relating to social inclusion, social cohesion and social capital, and consider how care-giving relates to these. I consider different critiques of official discourses and the role of care-giving in relation to these.

Carers, citizens and the value of care

A recent 'Citizen Audit for Britain' was designed to collect data on citizen participation in England, Scotland and Wales (Pattie *et al.*, 2003).The designers of this audit aimed to collect information on all types of citizen participation, including what they referred to as 'unorthodox' political participation, such as taking part in direct action, as well more traditional forms of political activity, and taking part in voluntary activity. In the latter they included involvement in personal support networks such as shopping for neighbours or visiting old people, but explicitly *excluded* such activities carried out in relation to anyone who was part of the family. For these researchers, spending an hour with an elderly neighbour constitutes evidence of citizenship activity, but providing 24-hour care, seven days a week, for a partner disabled by dementia or a stroke does not. This definitional exclusion is based in normative assumptions of citizenship as something that takes place in the public sphere. Families do not constitute part of the public sphere so action within families cannot be understood to constitute an exercise of citizenship – even though official 'family policy' does contain significant expectations of the way in which parents should exercise their responsibilities in relation to the creation of responsible citizens: for example, in terms of parenting orders to ensure acceptable behaviour of children.

This construction of citizenship as concerned with action and engagement within the public sphere is widespread (see, for example, Rimmerman, 1998; van Gunsteren, 1998). Indeed the concept of 'civil society' is usually explicitly understood to exclude social relations within families. Thus, in spite of the significance of the notion of 'civility' in theories of civil society (Whitehead, 2002), someone could behave violently and abusively within their families, but still be considered an active citizen making a positive contribution to civil society because they are involved in some form of voluntary association, or they are an active participant in a neighbourhood forum or some other form of participatory decision making.

This concept of citizenship has been challenged by feminist political scientists and by social policy analysts considering the role played by women in contributing to the welfare of children as well as that of disabled and older people. They have suggested that by constructing citizenship as comprising action in 'the public interest' and explicitly not focused on the 'private lives' of families, normative understandings of citizenship are inherently gendered. Feminists such as Pateman (1992) have discussed the dilemma faced by women in determining whether they should argue for a 'gender neutral' conception of citizenship which in practice means seeking inclusion alongside men on the same terms as men, or whether they should assert women's difference from men and thus a recognition that women will express their citizenship differently. Lister (1997) argues that it is not helpful to argue *either* for women's inclusion in citizenship on the basis of their contributions to social relations within the private sphere, *or* for prioritising women's individual rights for personal autonomy. She concludes that we need to break free from binary distinctions between equality and difference, gender-neutral or gender-differentiated notions of citizenship and an ethic of justice versus an ethic of care. She sees in Tronto and Sevenhuijsen's de-gendering of an ethic of care, with an emphasis on 'an ability to adopt the standpoint of others, particularly that of relatively powerless groups or individuals' (p. 102) a way of achieving this.

In spite of the prevalence of care-giving, the fact that all humans need care at some stages of their lives, and the apparent significance attached to it by governments (for example, Department of Health, 1999) care-giving is devalued in contemporary Western societies. Both paid and unpaid caring is disproportionately carried out by those who are least powerful: women, people from minority ethnic groups, migrants and older people (see, for example, Harrington Meyer, 2000; Ehrenreich and Hochschild, 2002).When it is paid work it is poorly paid. Both paid and unpaid care work is undertaken in situations characterised by limited security, where people often experience little choice about how support might be provided, and in which models of voice and representation for those undertaking such work are poorly developed (Standing, 2001). From the perspective of lay care-givers, the devaluing of the work they do is evidenced in the failure of 'professional' care-givers to recognise their knowledge and expertise, to give attention to their own needs and to express interest in them as individuals. From the perspective of care-receivers this can often result in being forced into receiving care from someone they would not choose to identify as a 'carer', and being identified as a 'burden' in danger of undermining the health and independence of a family member.

Much of the analysis of the reasons for this devaluing of care has concentrated on the gendered and racialised characteristics of care-giving (for example, Lewis, 2001). Caring is seen as 'naturally' the province of women, in particular women of low social class or from 'other' ethnic groups, and consequently of lower value than the work carried out in the public sphere and which is seen to contribute directly to the prosperity of society. But Tronto has suggested an additional reason for this devaluing of care:

> the disdain of 'others' who do caring (women, slaves, servants) has been virulent in our culture. This dismissal is inextricably bound up with an attempt to deny the importance of care. Those who are powerful are unwilling to admit their dependence upon those who care for them. To treat care as shabby and unimportant helps to maintain the positions of the powerful vis-à-vis those who do care for them. (Tronto, 1993, p. 174)

We can see something of this in the response to care of some within the disability movement. This is not to argue that disabled people occupy a powerful position in society, but to recognise the power of a discourse that makes a binary distinction between independence and autonomy and which is dismissive of those seen to occupy a position of dependence *vis-à-vis* others. In this context those who already experience themselves as marginalised as a result of social organisation premised on the assumption of able-bodiedness can be reluctant to acknowledge the necessity of interdependence when asserting the importance of enabling increased autonomy. The rejection of care *per se* in favour of a rights-based approach to support for disabled people has sometimes been couched in terms which are dismissive both of care as a social good and of those who provide it – both paid and unpaid. For example, Richard Wood, one time Director of the British Council of Disabled People, wrote:

> Disabled people have never demanded or asked for care! We have sought independent living which means being able to achieve maximum independence and control over our lives. The concept of care seems to many disabled people a tool through which others are able to dominate and manage our lives (Wood, 1991, p. 199)

Disabled people have done much to challenge a perception of impairment as a personal tragedy. They have made disability visible and have demonstrated the importance of disabled people having a voice in decisions at both personal and political levels that affect their lives. They have pointed up the often oppressive nature of social policies and practices which have contributed to the social exclusion of disabled people (for example, Campbell and Oliver, 1996). But that has sometimes meant accepting the distinction evident in much government discourse on welfare that people are *either* dependent (on care) *or* autonomous, as a result of being able to control the support they need, for example by employing a support worker through direct payments. In official discourse 'dependent' = bad and 'autonomous' = good, and there is a similar tendency in some disabled people's analyses. A major benefit of direct payments from this perspective is that employing a personal assistant, who does many of the same tasks as might be undertaken by a care-giver, enables such tasks to be reconstructed as 'personal support'. For Sian Vasey (1996), being able to pay for the help she, and other disabled people, need is to become 'independent of those around us' (p. 87). In this formulation the existence of a financial transaction between disabled person and personal support worker enables the relationship through which support is provided to be ignored. Because independence is valued and care-giving is not, the interdependence which characterises all human life and which for everyone at some stage of their life is expressed through care, is not recognised.

Tom Shakespeare (2000) offers an alternative discourse within which to understand this issue – that of help and helpfulness. He recognises the value of the feminist ethic of care as a counterbalance to the independent living model advocated by the disability movement: 'There can be too much stress on independence and autonomy within disability rights discourse. There is a contradiction between the collectivism of the disability movement and the individualism of the proposed solution to care' (p. 76). He suggests that a social policy and practice that incorporates both the disability rights and the feminist ethic of care perspective offers the best hope for empowerment and inclusion, but he remains somewhat uncomfortable with a discourse of care.

From another perspective there have been critiques of the way in which the New Labour Government in the UK has constituted caring as an *obligation* rather than an *expression* of citizenship (Harris, 2002). Harris argues that the discourse of care within New Labour is embedded in a familial discourse that privileges traditional families as the 'cornerstone of a decent society' (Labour Party, 1997, p. 27). This familial discourse is somewhat at odds with the emphasis on work as a basis for citizenship (Barnes and Prior, 2000, ch. 4). Harris argues that by highlighting the role played by carers in supporting individuals, and saving the state money by so doing, this contributes to the sense that caring is a duty, something over which people have no choice and which has the character of what Jordan (1989) has termed compulsory altruism. Harris's argument has some important insights, such as the danger that the emphasis on caring as an obligation of citizenship can emphasise a model of citizenship based solely in active participation. However, it is itself based in a model of citizenship as 'conferring rights to resources' (p. 277), which is a limited notion of how we should understand citizenship and one which tends to emphasise a competitive 'either/or' citizenship: either the carer or the person receiving care.

Harris's argument also fails to encompass the morality of care-giving. It opposes rights and obligations and does not recognise the significance of ethic of care principles underpinning social relations. What Tronto (1993) defines as *attentiveness* is largely lacking from consideration and there is a sense that any notion of *responsibility* towards others is slightly embarrassing to acknowledge. In a way similar to the disability movement's assertion of 'rights not care' it is an argument that reflects liberal notions of individual autonomy rather than recognising the universal human need for care. None of the carers whose stories are told in this book spoke of care-giving as a duty imposed on them by the state, although they all assumed a responsibility for caring which was based in pre-existing relationships, promises made, expectations about motherhood or cultural assumptions about care and reciprocity in family life. These carers were well aware of the demands and difficulties of care-giving, of the failure of state services to offer the information, services and support that would make their lives easier, that passing over the task of care-giving to state agencies was not an option, or if it was would result in a worse experience for those they support. But this is rather different from constructing care-giving as an externally imposed obligation unrelated to the way in which carers construct their own sense of what constitutes ethical social relations.

A feminist ethic of care offers a different way of understanding the relation between obligation, responsibility and care from that offered by Harris. Both Tronto and Sevenhuijsen (2000) distinguish duty from responsibility. A relational ontology recognises that individuals can only exist because they are members of networks of care and responsibility and this has implications for the way in which we think about obligations to others: 'the moral subject in the discourse of care always already lives in a network of relationships in which s/he has to find balances between different forms of responsibility (for the self, for others and for the relationships between them)' (Sevenhuijsen, 2000, p. 10). This reflects more closely the way in which carers spoke about their lives and experiences. They accepted the responsibility for care in the context of the relationships in which they were engaged, and were also trying to find a way of balancing concern about the other, their relationship with the other, and care for themselves. The nature of the support they received or did not receive from state agencies could make a significant difference to the effectiveness of that balancing act. This supports the findings of the Care Values and the Future of Welfare (CAVA) research that: 'Far from the dystopian vision of self-seeking individualism and moral decline which fills public debate…[people] are seeking to create new moral frameworks in which "fairness" to and "respect" for others are key aspirations' (Williams, 2004, p. 41).

Thus we should not reject the notion of *responsibility* to one another as evidence of a Third Way plot to force a moral awareness on us. Where the implementation of Third Way policies can be critiqued is in seeking to impose normative expectations about the precise contexts and forms the expression of such responsibilities should take, and in failing to support the type of practice and support services which can enable those involved in caring relationships to negotiate the shifting balances those relationships involve (see Chapter 9 and Jordan and Jordan, 2000).

Julia Twigg's (1989) analysis of the ways in which carers are conceptualised by service providers is also relevant here. In commenting on the first model she identified – that of carers as resources, with social care agencies fulfilling a residual role in those cases where lay care is either absent or ineffective – I wrote elsewhere:

> action on the part of social care agencies intended to make carers feel recognised and valued could help nudge this resource into a position in which it is more amenable to command. Hence, demonstrating goodwill and openness to influence from carers could be seen as a strategy for enhancing influence over carers. (M. Barnes, 1997, p. 125)

Twigg's second model of carers as 'co-workers' contains similar colonising potential. Agencies conceptualising carers in this way view them as quasi-professionals (Bond, 1992) and as colleagues working alongside paid workers in the support of their disabled or older relative. This can be seen as a precursor to the appeal to 'partnership' that has become a dominant theme within welfare discourse under New Labour.

Tronto (1993) argues that responsibility has both a different context and connotation to obligation: the former is more of a sociological and the latter a political concept. 'Responsibility is a term that is embedded in a set of implicit cultural practices, rather than in a set of formal rules or series of promises' (pp. 131–2). Not only does the notion of formal obligation fail to recognise the way in which care-giving and care-receiving are social practices which have to be negotiated in specific contexts in ways that are appropriate and responsive to that context, there is a danger that the existence of a contract to provide care will be mistaken for the actual experience of receiving care – that 'taking care of' rather than 'care-giving' will be evident. This is borne out in the stories of carers told in this book.

Caring, justice and social cohesion

Binary distinctions between rights and care, and those which separate care-providers from care-recipients, do not reflect the fluid identities and experiences of those involved in caring relationships. A social policy which is always weighing the interest of care-givers and care-receivers as separate is in danger of reinforcing a view of society as comprising isolated individuals in competition with each other for social goods. We need an approach to social justice capable of incorporating care as well as rights if we are to develop policies and practices capable of encompassing the circumstances both of disabled and older people and those who care for them. Because most of us experience being cared for and giving care at some stages in our lives, such an approach can have broad direct benefit. But because it is based in an understanding of the universality of human inter-relatedness it is not solely concerned with addressing the welfare of needy others.

Fraser (1997) argues for a view of social justice which integrates the importance both of redistribution and recognition. The absence of recognition is clearly part of the experience of injustice experienced by disabled people, older people and those who live with mental health problems. Fraser includes in her definition of 'cultural or symbolic injustice': 'disrespect (being routinely maligned or disparaged in stereotypic public cultural representations and/or in everyday life interactions)' (p. 14). Whilst carers may not experience such disrespect directly, they are personally affected by the lack of recognition and the disrespect experienced by those they care for. Fraser defines socioeconomic injustice as: 'rooted in the political-economic structure of society. Examples include exploitation (having the fruits of one's labor appropriated for the benefit of others); economic marginalization (being confined to undesirable or poorly paid work or being denied access to income-generating labor altogether), and deprivation (being denied an adequate material standard of living)' (p. 13). Both carers and those they help can experience both marginalisation and deprivation.

Fraser argues that remedies capable of addressing both the redistributive and recognition elements of social justice are those which are concerned with transformation. Such remedies do more than affirm the value of groups which are currently devalued, they deconstruct existing identities so that they 'not only raise the self-esteem of members of currently disrespected groups; they would change *everyone's* sense of self.' (p. 24, emphasis in the original). They avoid the danger that 'affirmative redistribution' not only does little to address the fundamental structures that generate disadvantage, but also can generate hostility to those groups targeted for assistance.

In the context of my current argument, the first danger to be avoided is that a binary distinction between care-giver and care-receiver can generate hostility if one or the other is targeted for specific attention and assistance. Both are implicated in the injustices of both distribution and recognition associated with age, disability, chronic illness, and in the provision of care. Part of the work of care-giving is to challenge the disrespect and lack of recognition experienced by those who receive care. Another is ensuring that entitlements to services and financial assistance are realised. But, as I have previously argued and as others have also demonstrated as a result of research with both carers and those receiving care (Henderson and Forbat, 2002), care-giver and care-receiver are not fixed identities which can *in fact* distinguish one group of people from another. The application of an ethic of care perspective which unsettles the notion of care-givers and care-receivers as distinct, and of care as something relevant only in situations where one person can be defined as needy and the other has responsibility for meeting that need, reinforces Fraser's advocacy of an approach to justice which is not focused on action directed solely at ameliorating the situation of an already disadvantaged and stigmatised group, but of transforming the way in which such disadvantage and stigmatisation is produced. We need to understand and challenge the way in which particular groups are singled out and constructed as needy and dependent, others are constructed as responsible for delivering care, and the needs of both are regarded as distinct from those of the 'independent majority' who have no need to be attentive to or take responsibility for others in their daily lives.

This also requires looking outward from the private world in which care is usually understood to operate, to reflect on the significance of care in the context of broader social relations. Contemporary policy discourses emphasise community, social inclusion, social cohesion and social capital – sometimes referred to as the 'glue' that binds societies together. In this context the preparedness of families and friends to provide unpaid support is seen not only as saving the state a considerable amount of money, but also as building and sustaining community, and limiting social exclusion. We have seen in the carers' stories told here how this can operate within individual caring relationships, but the collective work that care does for communities has been given much less attention than the work of caring for particular individuals.

Recognition of the significance of such roles is also germane to an understanding of women's contribution to building social capital. Putnam's (1993) influential work on the significance of social capital in creating societies that are not only socially cohesive, but also economically successful, has been subject to a number of critiques, including that of ignoring the significance of gender. Lowndes (2000) notes the way in which analyses of social capital which draw on membership of associations disregard the social networks in which women are involved as child carers: 'Such networks are produced and reproduced through a range of familiar activities, some characterised by mutuality, others by reciprocity – for instance, the 'school run', childcare 'swaps', baby-sitting, shared children's outings, emergency care, and the taking and fetching and watching of children in *their* school and club activities' (p. 534). We can extend this analysis to the role of family members and others in relation to the care of other relatives and the informal exchanges which take place in the context of this, leading in some instances to the establishment of more or less formal 'support groups'.

As we have seen, experiences of giving and receiving care need to be understood not only within personal histories but also within particular cultural contexts. White feminist critiques of care did not resonate with the lives and experiences of many black families – not only because of different notions of family within different cultures, but also because the provision of care within families was experienced as making a positive contribution to challenging the oppression experienced from outside the family. hooks' (1984) critique of white feminist analyses of motherhood and caring points to a different way of constructing 'care' – as part of a process through which people can challenge oppressions through solidarity within kinship groups. Stanlie James (1993) identifies 'othermothering' in black communities in the diaspora not only as a source of care for children whose parents were not in a position to look after them, but also as: 'powerful non-traditional resources utilized to intervene creatively in situations or conditions that threatened the survival of the community' (p. 51). She distinguishes the activities of females for their biological offspring which constitute Western notions of mothering from the 'cultural work' which may be undertaken by other blood and non-blood kin in West African and African American communities and which offers a much broader conceptualisation of mothering. She locates this in a culture in which reproduction was highly regarded, in which women were integrated into the economic activities which sustained the community and which 'were characterized by high degrees of interdependence and the belief that individual self-development and personal fulfilment were dependent upon the well-being of all members of the community' (p. 46).

Dixon-Fyle (2002) also highlights the social protection and welfare functions of extended families in traditional African societies, but argues that this is being undermined as a result of increased migration, the impact of AIDS and development policies which are out of kilter with local values and ethics. The emergence of AIDS as a devastating disrupter of family life has also created new needs for care-giving. In Southern Africa, community survival is threatened and the creative solutions which can be offered by family members, friends and neighbours to the provision of care and support is vital not only to individuals but to communities as a whole (Harber, n.d.).

In other social and cultural contexts, what can be described as caregiving within the frame offered by the ethic of care also demonstrates the centrality of this to both individual and collective well-being. For example, a study by Waller and Patterson (2002) of 'natural helping' in a Dinee (Navajo) community in Arizona found that helping kin was a central aspect of both individual and community identity, with little social distance between helpers and recipients. There was an absence of any clear distinction between categories of friend, neighbour or relative, and helpers were just as likely to support those we might call neighbours as kin. The researchers argue that not only does such helping express the interconnectedness of kin and non-kin within the community and act to maintain a positive identity, it is also a resource which enables individuals to learn how to become more resilient in situations in which they are faced with problems relating to poverty, alcohol use, illness and old age.

But in spite of the relevance of care to policies and practices concerned with the way in which we live together in communities, the concept of care is largely lacking from the policy discourses which promote more collective solutions to social problems. In various ways the New Labour Government's neighbourhood renewal strategy (SEU, 2001), the civil renewal strategy promoted from within the Home Office (Blunkett, 2003a and b) and policy initiatives relating to social exclusion and health improvement (for example, Department of Health, 1997) seek to develop greater solidarity and collective awareness of social problems and how they might be addressed, but do not use the concept of care in the way in which this is expressed. Rather they talk about 'capacity', 'empowerment', 'rights and responsibilities', 'duty and obligation', 'mutuality' and 'common purpose'.

Interestingly care does feature in the way in which young people talk about their understanding of the responsibilities of citizenship.

From a study of the way in which young people between 16 and 23 talked about what citizenship meant to them, and what constituted 'good' and 'bad' citizens, Lister *et al.* (2003) concluded that the most common construction of a 'good' citizen was someone who had: 'a considerate and caring attitude towards others and a constructive approach towards and active participation in the community' (p. 244).

In the context of a critique of Giddens' analysis of the normative framework of the *Third Way*, Sevenhuijsen (2000) argues the value of a care framework which acknowledges that individuals can exist only *because* they are members of various networks of care and responsibility. This contrasts with Giddens's view that the task for government is to build bridges *between* individuals and society. This is grounded in an influential analysis of contemporary society as characterised by an overwhelming process of 'individualisation' (Bauman, 2001; Beck and Beck-Gernsheim, 2002) and results in an analysis of the 'problem' faced by government as being the unwillingness of people to take responsibility for individual and collective well-being. In the context of some policy discourses, in particular that of the UK government's civil renewal agenda, this results in exhortations to citizens to act collectively out of duty to each other and the state. Paradoxically, when it comes to policy initiatives relating to care, the government itself encourages a view of this as an individualised activity, un-located in any broader notion of 'caring communities' (Department of Health, 1999)

Mackay's (1998) analysis of the views and experiences of Scottish women politicians suggests that the absence of care from much policy discourse results from gendered processes of policy making. She suggests men's unawareness of issues of care means they have difficulty in dealing with the complexities of many social problems. Because women politicians' everyday experiences are of negotiating and reconciling the value of care, relationships and family life with the decisions they have to reach about policy issues, they are more able to understand the relationship between 'common sense' understandings of care and care as a political and moral principle.

Mackay's argument that the absence of care from political discourse is associated with the limited presence of women in political decision making should not be taken to mean that it is women's responsibility to introduce care into decision making. Rather the fact that care *has* been regarded as (and experienced as) gendered is one reason why its significance has not been acknowledged. Tronto has argued that men in powerful positions fail to acknowledge the caring work that has and continues to sustain their lives – something she refers to as 'privileged irresponsibility' (1993, p. 112). Key arguments for an ethic of care as a basis for social policy decision making are: firstly, that *everyone* should be guaranteed access to both the giving and receiving of care (Sevenhuijsen, 2000) and thus that women and men should have time for care (Williams, 2004); and secondly; the assumption that humans are interdependent is an important starting point for a range of areas of policy making, including health care, employment policy and community development, as well as social care.

Deliberating with care

A care perspective recognises that not all citizens are equal, but that the achievement of equality is a political goal (Tronto, 1993). It does not seek to *replace* a rights perspective, but argues that this is not enough to achieve justice in conditions in which humans exist in a condition of interdependence. Such interdependence implies a conception of 'needs' that understand these as 'necessarily intersubjective, cultural, rather than individual' (ibid., p. 164). It is essential to recognise that there are different levels of need to be met if socially just outcomes are to be achieved (Morris, 2001) and such recognition comes from an application of the four moral principles of care.

But a care perspective also has implications for the nature of the democratic processes necessary to achieve socially just outcomes. Deliberative practices which enable dialogue about experiences deriving from the disadvantage and marginalisation resulting from disability, old age or mental distress, and from experiences of giving and receiving care, can encourage attentiveness to such experiences and give recognition to them (see, for example, Barnes, 2002b; 2004; Barnes *et al.*, forthcoming). The evidence of direct testimony from older people, people with mental health problems and others often regarded as incompetent or lacking in capacity makes it hard to continue to ignore their individual and collective agency. The process of attending to voices that may be expressed in ways other than is usual in official policy contexts and which demand a response because of the substance of what is said, can encourage a preparedness to take responsibility to act to ameliorate the situations being described. Such attentiveness also highlights when a lack of competence is evident in the way in which support services are provided, as well as the response of those on the receiving end of services to the nature of the care and support provided. The difficulties officials can experience in engaging in face-to-face dialogue with people who may be angry or upset by the way in which they have been treated, or whose styles of communication are very different from what they are familiar with in official deliberations, force them to confront their own competence in relating to others who are different from them (Church, 1996).

It is harder to ignore the significance of the moral principles of an ethic of care in circumstances where there is face-to-face dialogue with people whose everyday lives are suffused with the experience of giving and receiving care, although there is also evidence from the practices that exist in some deliberative forums that this cannot be taken for granted (Barnes *et al.*, 2004). As I noted in Chapter 2, the validity of narrative as expressing a reality to which service providers and policy makers need to respond is not always acknowledged. A care perspective could enhance the capacity of such forums to generate outcomes that achieve social justice for marginalised groups, assist in developing a vocabulary through which care can be integrated into dialogues about policies and services, as well as encouraging an understanding of the significance of care beyond the context of relations between 'caring' and 'needy' people.

Collective action amongst carers demonstrates the way care is given and received within such groups. Similarly, mental health service user organisations, disabled people's and older people's groups demonstrate care for group members as well as engaging in individual and collective advocacy on their behalf. Here, the achievement of justice by attaining both recognition and redistribution is bound up with a process of caring for each other. What is required is more opportunity for deliberation which recognises that identities as 'disabled people' or 'carers' are constructed within particular discourses that make life easier for service providers rather than reflecting the lived experiences of those involved in caring relationships. Rather than constructing dialogue with service users or with carers about services solely in terms of consultation about specific proposals (where the key decisions have already been made), we should understand such dialogue as opportunities for an exploration of how such identities are constructed, what they mean for those concerned, how people negotiate their identities and relationships in the context of their everyday lives, and what are the consequences of this for the development of socially just policies and practices. This is something the disability movement has had considerable success in. Their articulation of the social model of disability has influenced practices, policies and services in a way that emphasises the citizenship of disabled people. Similarly, older people's movements have challenged ageist policies based in a view of old age as a period of inevitable decline. We need something similar which can address not only the meaning that care has for people in the context of their one-to-one relationships, but how caring values can inform the decisions about policies which shape the circumstances in which people live their lives.

Conclusion

Most research on the subject of care focuses on the problems and burdens associated with individual care-giving, and most discussions of care understand it in this context. In spite of contemporary policy discourses that utilise a range of concepts to express aspirations towards a greater connectedness between members of diverse communities, care is largely invisible in such discourses. This reflects the way in which the significance of care in all human relationships is hidden, and the way in which care has come to be associated with an absence of autonomy and with disempowerment. But care-giving makes a significant contribution to social well-being and to the achievement of social justice – not only directly through the support received by particular individuals which can contribute to their capacity to resist oppression and to participate in social life, but also by offering practical examples of an ethical basis for social relations which recognise equality as an objective to be achieved.

CHAPTER 9

Caring Practices: Ethics and Narratives

In this final chapter I address the implications of my analysis for the practice of those who work directly with those involved in caring relationships. I argue both for the advantages of a narrative life history approach capable of delivering a practice that understands care giving and receiving in the context of individual and shared histories, and that a feminist ethic of care can provide the moral principles underpinning practices sensitive to both care and justice. In UK social policy, formal rights of those receiving social care and health services are defined within broad legal frameworks such as the Human Rights Act, specific legal provisions such as the Health and Social Care Act and the Mental Health Act, and within the procedural rules and guidance produced by statutory agencies responsible for delivering such care. Practitioners are guided by professional ethical codes which usually articulate a general statement of the values that underpin practice and may offer guidance about how to respond in certain types of situation (Banks, 2001, p. 88). Both legal frameworks and professional codes aspire to ensure that the practice of social and health care contributes to social justice objectives. But the complexity of the circumstances of individual service users and their families, and the dilemmas they face in seeking to enable the autonomy of the service user without the abuse of the carer, is often such that precise guidance and formal rules are neither possible, sufficient nor helpful as a means of ensuring the achievement of such objectives (Brannelly, 2004). As Dominelli (2002) has argued, such principles are expressed in a way that ignores the particular social context in which problems and dilemmas are experienced.

Care and ethics

The moral principles embodied within a feminist ethic of care can act
as a guide to different forms of practice, including social work, domiciliary and personal care and nursing (Brannelly, 2004). They do not
prescribe a precise form of practice nor define procedural guidelines
to be followed. Ethic of care principles draw attention to the need to
focus care on the care-receiver, the care-giver and on the relationship
between them. Good care requires a continual negotiation between
those providing and those receiving care. An approach based in an
ethic of care can accommodate the range of care-providers involved,
particularly in complex circumstances, because it is based in the social
relations of care, and values reciprocity in the process of giving and
receiving care.

An important argument for developing social care practices based
on ethic of care principles is the potential for effective dialogue
between paid and lay carers. Warren (1990) addressed the way in
which paid home-helps blurred the boundaries between work and
friendship relationships as a result of the moral qualities with which
their work came to be imbued. Stone (2000) discusses tensions between
the ideals of 'good care' defined by paid care-givers and what organisations expect care to consist of. Justice and fairness in care-giving are
also defined rather differently by care-givers and formal organisations,
according to Stone. Her analysis of findings from a number of
research projects emphasises the similarities between ideas of good
care in different contexts: including care provided in an institutional
context and that provided in people's own homes, and identifies the
way in which such care is compared with care by families in order to
define 'good care'. Even though paid care workers acknowledge that
family care can be bad, incompetent or even abusive:

> For every kind of caring work in the public sphere, there is an
> analogue in the private sphere that hovers around as a kind of inspi-
> rational doppelganger...Caregivers and care recipients seem to
> carry images of this other sphere and use them to compare and
> judge caring in the public sphere. (p. 94).

The characteristics that appear to distinguish 'caring' from 'doing a
job' from the perspective of the diverse care workers in the studies she
reviewed are: listening and talking, rather than carrying out tasks with-

out words; emotional attachment rather than detachment; a capacity to reconcile the moral imperatives of treating all service users equally whilst responding to the uniqueness of each person; spending time building up trust, rather than prioritising sticking to the schedule; being able to go beyond the boundaries of a professional or employment relationship; working through relationships rather than rules: seeing company and friendship as a priority.

We can relate these characteristics to the ethic of care principles elaborated by Tronto:

1. *Listening and talking.* Attentiveness to the needs of others requires an other-directed active listening. A failure to explore and understand the precise circumstances of lay care-givers and service users can be considered 'wilful ignorance' (Tronto, 1993, p. 129) when this failure is evident amongst those whose job it is to provide help. 'Carrying out procedures', such as working through an assessment schedule without actively listening to what is said, how this is said, and what is not said, can amount to inattentiveness. But talk can be just as important to attentiveness. Appropriate responses to the words of others reflect the attention that needs to be given to what is and what is not said. Enabling others to talk and thus helping the helper to learn about their needs and circumstances is a key task.

2. *Emotional attachment rather than detachment.* The significance of emotional attachment in the context of an ethic of care goes beyond recognising that emotional labour is an element of care. Warren wrote: 'Just as home helps found themselves doing tasks which they had not anticipated would be part of their work, so they felt responsibility for old people in ways, or to an extent, they had not expected. In general, women were not prepared for what they described as their "involvement" with elderly people' (1990, p. 78). Responsibility – understood in a sociological or anthropological rather than philosophical or political context – is a core principle of an ethic of care. From this perspective, responsibility should not be understood as a set of formal rules which workers are obliged to implement, but rather as a relational concept out of which different care practices can be developed which are sensitive and appropriate to the particular situation. Brannelly (2004) highlighted the way in which practitioners (social workers and CPNs) working with people with dementia who created a distance

between themselves and the person with whom they were working demonstrated a *lack* of responsibility when they made decisions about care that they knew to be unacceptable to the person concerned. Dominelli (2002) has argued that anti-oppressive practice requires workers who are able to integrate skills in practice, intellect and emotions. Care is not simply an emotional disposition towards another, but involves accepting responsibility to act. Assuming responsibility to act on the basis of an attentiveness to the particularities of needs of service users and family carers requires the capacity to 'judge with care', not from the perspective of a detached set of rules and procedures, but in relation to a particular social and cultural circumstance.

3. *Reconciling equal treatment with uniqueness.* Recognition of the uniqueness of the situations of each service user and family carer requires attentiveness. The capacity to be attentive to uniqueness and also to recognise and respond to the range of needs and circumstances that a worker has to support and help is another way in which judging with care is required. Underpinning this criterion for 'good care' in the research reviewed by Stone was the acknowledgment that workers had 'favourites' amongst those they helped. But amongst the stories of family carers explored in this book we have evidence that it is not necessary to love or even like someone in order to be attentive to their uniqueness and to treat them with respect and dignity. Alan surprised his siblings by saying his care for his mother was not motivated by love, but by a promise he made to her. But this did not prevent him from trying to ensure that the care she received, both from himself and paid care workers, responded not only to her physical needs but also to her need for personal integrity. An ethic of care recognises the reality of inequality, individuality and diversity. It does not resolve the dilemma of the infinite need for care and how limited resources are allocated in response to need. But it does alert us to the danger of understanding needs as a commodity that can be met by the allocation of a precise quantity of another commodity – care. By emphasising care as a relational practice in which we are all implicated, and justice as not just an issue of distribution, but also of recognition, a feminist ethic of care acknowledges that messy moral dilemmas are an inevitable part of caring relationships involving paid workers as well as lay care-givers.

4. *Spending time and building up trust.* Tronto argues that retreating into

a professional code of ethics should not be permitted as a way of enabling individuals to escape responsibility for incompetence in doing their job because if they fail to provide good care, then the need for care will not be met. Another way of looking at this is that service users and carers will not trust paid workers who perform incompetently, and arguing that workers are following an abstract code of practice will be an inadequate defence. In this context Tronto also locates her distinction between 'taking care of', that is, putting in place systems, processes and personnel intended to meet a need, and 'care giving' – the actual process of meeting the need. One example of this is systems which exist for providing adaptations to the homes of disabled people being unable to deliver within a time period, which indicates to the carers that their needs and the needs of those they support are not being met. Brannelly's study of social workers and CPNs working with people with dementia offers another perspective on this. Workers who were able to build up a relationship over a long period of time were more likely to pay regard to the outcomes of care processes, not least because they were able to build up a picture of the person themselves which they could use to evaluate the suitability and effectiveness of care provision. CPNs were more likely than social workers to be able to do this because the emphasis in social workers' workloads was on the initial assessment process, and assessing the *outcomes* of care was seen as secondary.

5. The remaining criteria for good care identified through Stone's work all refer to the significance of relationships: going beyond the boundaries of professional or employment relationships; working through relationships rather than rules; and seeing company and friendship as a priority. These all emphasise the importance of determining appropriate responses through attentiveness to the particular context and what this means for those involved. They also emphasise the interactive nature of care: a relationship implies the participation of at least two people. In defining *responsiveness* as the fourth moral principle underpinning an ethic of care, Tronto highlights the significance of acknowledging that at least one of those involved in a caring relationship is likely to be more vulnerable than the other. Whilst no individual is entirely autonomous and self-supporting, the caring relationships which are the subject of this book involved one person who was more in

need of support than the other. Tronto identifies the particular 'moral moment' (p. 134) related to this as the responsiveness of the care-receiver to care in conditions of vulnerability and inequality. This is an important distinction from the way in which the notion of responsiveness is commonly used in the context of the relationship between paid and unpaid care workers and those they support. It is more usual to talk about the carer *responding* to the needs of the care-receiver. In Tronto's analysis this is encompassed by the notion of *attentiveness*. By including the response of the care-receiver in this way Tronto emphasises that the vulnerability of the care-receiver is not an excuse for paternalism (or maternalism), nor for assuming that we can interpret the care-receiver's response as if it were our own: 'Responsiveness suggests a different way to understand the needs of others rather than put ourselves into their position. Instead it suggests that we consider the other's position as that other expresses it. Thus, one is engaged from the standpoint of the other, but not simply by presuming that the other is exactly like the self.' (p. 136)

The tensions between what front-line paid care-givers and care organisations regard as the responsibilities of care workers and their conceptualisations of good care are played out in the day-to-day negotiations between workers and service users, and in the lives of the workers themselves as they struggle to accommodate what they feel they ought to do with what their employers tell them they should and should not do. The ways in which care workers define what they understand as good care are more in line with the moral principles of an ethic of care and more consistent with the way in which lay care-givers talk about care than with highly task-oriented procedural approaches. For the home-helps in Warren's (1990) study, and the women providing child care in their own homes studied by Tuominem (2000), the work they do is both socially valuable and important to them. Tuominem suggests that an understanding of the socially constructed nature of an ethic of care enables us to understand better how 'the call to serve the community and its members' (p. 133) contributes to a valued social identity which embraces both their care for their own families and for others' children.

Warren suggests that the home-helps she studied faced a 'double bind' as the close relationship between their roles at home and at work meant that if they were found wanting at work this called into question their 'natural' capacities as carers. This stresses the importance of de-coupling an ethic of care from essentialist notions of the 'natural' nurturing role and capacity of women, but Stone, Tuominem and Warren's work also challenges the dualism which attempts to dislocate what are typically regarded as the private moral principles of care from the public virtues of professional and paid work. Traustadottir's (2000) study of women caring for disabled children in the family, as friends, and in human service organisations, found remarkable similarity in the care work in each of these three domains. Such work included: (1) *Caring for*: including preparing meals, providing personal care, planning outings, keeping in touch with relatives, and more 'professional' care such as therapy and treatment. Much of this work was directed towards ensuring the acceptance of the disabled child within her/his social networks. (2) *Caring about*: the significance of love and emotional closeness meant that it was hard for mothers, workers and friends to distinguish between the activities and emotions involved in caring. (3) *Extended caring*: some of the women caring in all three domains went beyond the personal care they provided to specific disabled children and expressed their care about disabled people in general, for example through becoming advocates lobbying government officials and service providers. Both the first and third of these types of care reflect the integration between care and justice in both the purpose and practice of care-giving in some situations. This was also evident in the care-givers whose stories are told in this book.

My argument is not that the help provided by paid workers – whether social workers, domiciliary care workers, nurses or others – is or should be indistinguishable from that provided by family members and friends. There are particular professional skills as well as knowledge that lay care-givers and those they support can benefit from and have a right to expect. Nor is it right to suggest that the paid work undertaken by workers employed to help people should be similarly unbounded as that undertaken by lay care-givers. Women are particularly susceptible to arguments to make commitments over and above those required for their job, and can experience considerable tension and conflict in the various demands that are made on them in the context of working and family life. The home-helps in Warren's study found the rules governing their involvement in their work important because of this: 'Flesh and blood come first', as one explained it (p. 78). In the case of workers involved primarily in 'body work' – bathing and other forms of intimate care – the use of gloves whilst bathing service users not only provides a physical protection from the possibility of, for example, getting faeces under the fingernails, but also serves a symbolic purpose: 'Gloves were used by workers to protect themselves from the full intimacy of bathing work and to put up a barrier of professionalism between the client and the worker' (Twigg, 2000, p. 151).

It is perhaps important to make a distinction between boundaries in terms of the *quantity* of input that can be reasonably expected and the nature of the care-giving process and the relationship within which support is provided. It is neither reasonable nor fair to expect paid workers to be 'on call' and available at any time to attend to the needs of service users. (But neither is it fair to expect lay carers to be available at all times.) Nor is it possible or appropriate to suggest that the relationship between paid helper and service user is the same as that between, for example, a mother and her disabled daughter, a son and his chronically ill mother, or a woman and her husband with dementia. The key issue is how the job of helping is carried out within a different set of boundaries from those that apply in lay care-giving relationships. Bathing assistants may wear gloves when a mother, son or wife would not, but this does not mean they cannot be attentive, responsible, competent and aware of the response of the service user to the usual bounds of privacy being broken because of their need for help. A social worker may not be able to drop in every week for a chat with an elderly service user whose care package they are co-ordinating. But that does not mean that when they do discuss what help is needed and how it may be provided they cannot demonstrate similar qualities. This brief example can serve as an illustration. Judith Okely is describing an incident involving her mother, thought by doctors to have Alzheimer's disease, but who was subsequently found to have been infected with new-variant CJD:

> The visiting social worker showed brilliant initiative. At first, Bridget refused to come out of her room to meet him. Finally, she appeared in her dressing gown. She continued to remonstrate. I slipped in somewhere that my mother had once been a social worker. My mother recalled her overall responsibility for the elderly in an entire London Borough in the 1950s. The social worker then asked if, in her past experience, she would have thought it right to check up on someone who had just had a major operation. Bridget got the point, giggled, agreed and made friends. (Okely, 1999, p. 40)

Thus what I am suggesting is that the moral principles of attentiveness, responsibility, competence and responsiveness offer a perspective within which it is possible to consider what constitutes 'good care' provided by paid and unpaid care-givers, and that this creates a shared language within which lay and paid carers and service users can discuss the support that is necessary in any particular situation and how this should be provided. This shared language is one which could enable conversations about the practical support needed to make everyday life possible: such as the provision of aids and adaptations; the personal and intimate help provided, for example, to enable disabled people to take a bath; the nursing care necessary to deal with the physical symptoms of illness; the relief which enables lay care-givers to take time for themselves; and the help needed to renegotiate relationships which can become highly stressful.

However, there is evidence to suggest that such conversations are all too rare. Pickard and Glendinning (2002) suggest that, even when lay carers evidence considerable expertise based on substantial experience of providing care, and when there is a substantial overlap in the precise types of care provided by family members and by nurses, it is more accurate to describe paid and family carers as working in a complementary fashion rather than working together, and some workers appear to be reluctant to talk directly about the help that is necessary, and how this might be given. Of the carers I spoke to for this project, only Rose spoke of a dialogue with paid care workers in which there was a sense that they were sharing knowledge and experience within a framework of shared values concerning care.

Brannelly's (2004) study demonstrated the inadequacy of formal notions of justice deriving from the Human Rights Act as a basis for defining social practices that are both just and caring in the context of work with people with dementia. She argued that models and principles of citizenship used by other groups of service users who have actively campaigned for their citizenship are not beneficial in this case. Whilst the position of people with dementia does raise particular dilemmas concerning notions of empowerment and citizenship, the limitations of a rights-based approach extend beyond its application to this group of service users. Jenny Morris, a feminist also active within the disability movement who has argued powerfully *for* a rights-based approach to disability issues and challenged able-bodied writers addressing family care from a feminist perspective, has acknowledged the need to include an ethics of care perspective alongside the social model of disability, in order to promote the human rights of disabled people. She writes:

> We need an ethics of care which is based on the principle that to deny the human rights of our fellow human beings is to undermine our own humanity. We need an ethics of care which recognises that anyone – whatever their level of communication or cognitive impairment – can express preferences. We need an ethics of care which aims to enable people to participate in decisions that affect them and to be involved in the life of their community. Most importantly, we need an ethics of care which, while starting from the position that everyone has the same human rights, also recognizes the additional requirements that some people have in order to access those human rights. The recognition of our difference (including our dependence), because of our impairments, can thus become a passport to the recognition of our common humanity. (2001, p. 15)

She illustrates her argument with an example of a young man with severe cognitive and communication impairments whose life was transformed when he started attending a day centre and experienced a care relationship which 'started with his human right to communicate and which sought ways to make this possible' (ibid., p. 14).

In the next section I develop ideas about the way in which a value-based approach embedded in a feminist ethics of care can be implemented through a practice that employs a narrative methodology.

Constructing and re-constructing narratives

The design of support services in the absence of any biographical or relationship contextualisation is common. In Chapter 2 I discussed life-history work with people with learning difficulties which had been developed to counteract the dominant tendency for care plans to adopt an a-historical, purely functional approach to determining services. In this section I want to suggest that narratives can serve two purposes in working with disabled or older service users and with lay care-givers: they can help practitioners find out about and *understand* current circumstances in the context of individual and shared histories and relationships, and in the context of broader social and cultural circumstances, thus enabling caring practices to be shaped to the particularities of specific circumstances; and narrative can be a *process* through which practitioners, carers and service users can collaborate to create opportunities for change and improvement in their circumstances.

I have identified listening and talking as one criterion for good care and one that can be related to the moral principle of attentiveness. This can be understood as attentiveness to the particularity of the person needing help, a particularity based in their history and current relationships through which their identity has been and continues to be constructed. Brannelly's research identified that attentiveness was helped when practitioners had an awareness of the biography of the person with dementia. This allowed them to find out about preferences for care, what was and what was not acceptable to the person. She writes:

> Biographical understanding by the practitioner of the person with dementia was built over time, and practitioners who had a greater understanding had been involved with people with dementia over a longer period of time. This also allowed the person with dementia to develop a 'feel' for the practitioner, recognising them, but maybe not knowing their name or what their work entailed. Practitioners were attentive to other problems that the person with dementia found important in their lives, and worked to support them through various difficulties such as marital problems and diagnosis of cancer (Brannelly, 2004, p. 289).

She also noted that knowledge of the biography of the person with dementia was linked to an explicit regard and respect for the person. Knowing about and understanding the roles people had developed throughout their lives made it easier for practitioners to see beyond their current impairments and to recognise both the person and the citizen. Here I develop a discussion of the type of listening and talking that can enable workers to be attentive to that identity and through this to understand the response of the service user to the help that is sought and offered.

Social care assessments are based on a set series of questions which require the practitioner to find out about a number of pre-defined functional states which have been decided to be important in order to determine an appropriate agency response, leading to the shorthand summarisation of a person's current state indicated by the extract from

my mother's case review (see Chapter 2). The assessor is in the position of a 'collector of information' from the service user and/or their
carer, and this information is treated as an objective description of
their emotional state, physical capacities, social and financial circumstances and current relationships which is sufficient to determine what
help they should receive. Both the way in which assessments are
carried out and their adequacy as a basis on which to build an empowering practice have been subject to a number of critiques (for example,
Marsh and Fisher, 1992; Ellis, 1993; Smale and Tuson, 1993; Davis,
Ellis and Rummery, 1997; Richards, 2000). Here my emphasis is on
distinguishing a process of *information collection* from that of *narrative
construction*.

Whilst the interviews carried out in preparation for this book were
not intended to be the basis of on-going work with lay carers or those
they supported, the approach I adopted to the interviews is illustrative
of constructivist approaches to social work (and other social practices)
capable of generating understanding and providing a basis for change.
My primary purpose was to understand what care-giving meant to
those I interviewed, and how they made sense of this experience in the
context of other aspects of their lives. I wanted to hear how carers
spoke about care-giving, how they told their stories, and to explore the
relationship between 'care' and 'justice' in the way in which they
discussed what had happened to the person they supported and the
impact that care-giving had had on their lives. I did not approach
carers with a pre-defined set of questions, but rather invited them to
tell me their story, starting where they wanted, and selecting what they
wanted to talk about. I did ask questions – but only in response to
issues they had brought up, because I was not clear about something,
or because there appeared to be some gap in their story. Sometimes a
carer's unwillingness to follow a lead I had suggested in such questions
served to emphasise the way in which they were constructing their own
meanings and determining what they thought was important in telling
their story.

Interestingly, in view of the main messages coming from much
research on care-giving, talk about the tasks of care-giving was often a
result of direct questions from me, rather than what carers themselves
selected to talk about. This is not to underestimate the importance of
the tasks of care-giving, nor their demanding nature. But it does
suggest that if carers are given the opportunity to talk openly about
care-giving, other aspects of the experience emerge as important in

terms of understanding not only what caring means, but also how this might be supported.

The stories were created – constructed – within a particular context. Carers were invited to tell their stories to someone known or introduced to them as working in a university department with responsibilities that included training social workers and other social care workers, as having demonstrated a commitment to carers through previous work with carers' groups, and as having had some personal experience as a result of my mother's dementia. The purpose was explicitly to contribute to the preparation of a book that could be used in training social care workers. Broadly this can be construed as a 'research' rather than 'practice' purpose. I was not aiming to intervene or achieve change in the lives of those I spoke to, although on this occasion, as on others when I have interviewed people for research purposes, it has appeared that the people I interviewed gained some satisfaction from telling their stories and receiving recognition for them. Undoubtedly stories would have been constructed and told differently if I had been identified as a service gatekeeper. The response sought by the teller would have been an immediate, practical one, rather than the delayed and uncertain response implied by the use of their stories for training purposes. Does this mean that the approach I adopted in generating narratives for this book is not relevant to practice?

As a researcher I am struck by the way in which texts that address constructivist or narrative approaches to practice engage with many similar issues of epistemology and method as texts discussing research practice. This is, or should be, unsurprising. Just as social practitioners are increasingly developing theoretical and methodological bases for practices that explicitly reflect the social rather than clinical nature of their activity (for example, Parton and O'Byrne, 2000; Folgheraiter, 2004), so too are social researchers asserting both a theoretical and methodological robustness based not in the rules of the physical sciences, but in the way in which meaning is constructed and social phenomena are constituted through discourse (for example, Alvesson and Skoldberg, 2000, ch. 6; Cameron, 2001). In both cases the role of language is vitally important. 'Telling our story is a way of reclaiming ourselves, our history and our experiences; a way of finding our voice. In telling my story to others I am also telling it to my "self" – and my "self" (who is the audience) is being formed in the process of telling' (Etherington, 2000, p.17). The practices of both social research and social care rely on language as a medium through which both information and meaning are communicated, and both require an active interpretation of what is said and exchanged. For the researcher this leads to an analysis that usually involves the consideration of a number of 'cases' in order to look for patterns, similarities and differences within and across 'cases', which enable new insights to be gained into social phenomena and offers the potential of contributing to social change. For the practitioner this process of interpretation is intended to lead to the development of a response or intervention designed to achieve change in a particular 'case'. In both cases participative approaches aim to ensure that the process of interpretation is a collaborative one. Such approaches recognise the significance of the experiential or local knowledge of the 'research subject' or 'service user', as well as the 'expert knowledge' of the researcher or practitioner.

We can now understand how a narrative approach can enable practitioners to achieve the attentiveness necessary to provide competent and responsive care. It is not simply a matter of 'finding out' factual information about the lives of service users and those who care for them, nor a process of carrying out functional assessments designed to allocate users to a dependency or risk category which triggers a predefined level of service input. Rather it is a process through which practitioners can get to know both users and carers, to understand something about the relationship between them, to be able to anticipate likely responses to different forms of intervention, and to suggest ways of working most likely to enable both users and carers to practise their citizenship. This is relevant to a variety of practices, including practical assistance such as the provision of aids and adaptations, and personal assistance such as the provision of bathing and other personal care. For example, a narrative of the daily lives of Rose and Arif as they care for Surya, carrying her downstairs every morning, with help from care assistants relieving the stiffness in her limbs and preparing her for school, in the context of their deep love for her, their enduring anxiety about her health and their sadness at the failure of other family members to recognise her personhood, is highly relevant to practitioners who have responsibilities both to assess for and to provide practical aids.

For practitioners who work more directly with the emotional aspects of the lives of service users and carers, who may be asked to help when relationships become strained or difficult, or whose intervention is sought to address issues concerning relationships between service users, lay carers and the social world, narrative can also serve another purpose. Parton and O'Byrne (2000) develop a detailed analysis of social work based in the constructive power of language to enable human beings to imagine and to do things. The process of reconstructing or 're-storying' lives or relationships that are problematic is in itself a means of starting to change and improve situations. It is an approach that assumes that people have significant resources, but it is in the way that these are 'storied' that is the key to opening up new and more positive possibilities in people's lives. Dominelli (2002) advocates a similar approach in relation to practice designed to be empowering and which understands the process of identity formation as a central focus. Practitioners who recognise the dynamic process of identity formation and are able to engage with service users in open discussion and negotiation about who they are and who they want to be are less likely to respond to people as stereotypes and more likely to both recognise and support service users as active agents.

The examples Parton and O'Byrne develop of the theory and practice of 'constructive social work' focus on work with children, with adolescents and with families. They identify other texts which address similar approaches in work with people with mental health problems, with substance abusers and other in contexts such as work with children in residential care, but there is only a passing reference to its possibilities in work with older people and none to work with disabled people. Does this mean that it is not relevant or appropriate in these circumstances?

Mattingly's (1998) studies of the work of occupational therapists with disabled people (see Chapter 2) suggests that there *is* a valuable role for therapeutic narratives in work with disabled people. There are also indications in the stories told in this book of family carers recognising the importance of constructing new stories about lives together and separately, and of new ways of living together in difficult circumstances. These relate both to their own identities as caregivers and to the identities of those they support. One example of this is Nell helping James to imagine a life for himself in which she is no longer able to be his friend and carer as well as his mother. This anticipation of the future and both drawing on and developing resources to live a differently imagined life requires the capacity to develop a plot in which the characters have different roles and relationships than in the present, but without this appearing threatening. It is a familiar plot to parents of able-bodied children, but one which has to be worked at and rediscovered when the usual expectations of the parent–child trajectory are disrupted by the birth of a disabled child. The successful development of such a plot can be greatly helped by the preparedness of social care practitioners to play an active role in this, and by the level of trust in social care services engendered through experience of their use. I remember from my work with carers' groups the frustration of mothers of disabled children about the absence of anticipatory discussions or planning which helped them prepare themselves and their children for the time when they would no longer be able to support them. And if the advice given to Nell when James's disability became evident had been followed (see page 55), the notion of an imagined future in which he would live on his own would have been inadmissible. Another perspective on this is illustrated by Rose's unwillingness to look beyond the immediate future and to imagine possibilities for Surya. At the time I spoke with her, her fear was that Surya would be left to die if she became ill, because doctors had questioned whether she would want her to be resuscitated. In such circumstances an absence of trust in service providers inhibits the possibility of collaborating to imagine a future and to prepare for this.

A rather different example of the way in which 're-storying' can play a part in ameliorating difficulties was evident in Alan's story. Alan spoke of the way in which his mother used the time when she was being cared for by him to reconstruct her identity as a good mother. Although his own experience and that of his siblings was very far from coinciding with this perception, he did not challenge her on this. Catherine's way of dealing with the disappointments of her life had previously been destructive (her drinking had been a way of dealing with the fact that her parents did not like her and her marriage was unhappy), but at this point in her life it was important for the two of them to find a way of living together which included times of peace and shared enjoyment which would make the difficult task of caregiving possible. Although Alan could not share in the re-construction of the historical experience of his relationship with his mother, Catherine's re-storying probably made it easier to share positive experiences at the end of her life and, perhaps because he (and probably she) knew that her life would not last much longer, it was possible to accept her reconstruction rather than challenge it. Alan's absence of trust in statutory service providers meant that he saw no place for them in addressing these interpersonal dimensions of the caring relationship in which they were involved. He was not prepared to 'explain' his siblings' reluctance to help him look after his mother and this in itself was part of his contribution to the re-storying process in which Catherine was engaged.

For Lise and Eric, his stroke came at a point in their lives when the power relations within their marriage were starting to shift. His need for her support required them to develop a new story of their lives together in which Lise took on roles, such as responsibility for financial planning, which had not characterised their previous relationship. Although Eric was not an easy man to care for, her role as individual carer enabled her to construct a positive identity as a woman strong enough not only to support her husband, but also to take on public roles advocating for older people and their carers.

This process of constructing and re-constructing narratives of lives together and separately in difficult circumstances can be considered a key dimension of the emotional labour of care-giving. It constitutes the 'constructive' and 're-constructive' care that Nolan *et al.* (1996) distinguish from the more functional dimensions of care-giving, and also contains aspects of the 'anticipatory' care which these authors also identify. The absence of explicit examples of such work in these contexts in key social work texts probably says more about the current priorities of social work in the UK than about the relevance of constructive social work to work with family carers and those they support. Certainly the social worker allocated to my mother appeared to have no role other than some form of co-ordination of other inputs. The social workers in Brannelly's (2004) study also had less of the on-going contact with older people with dementia than did CPNs, who were consequently able to build up a better understanding of their lives and preferences than were social workers. Narrative work with older people, people with learning difficulties and disabled people is usually reported as taking place in residential or day-care settings where, once again, long-term and often quite intensive contact between practitioners and service users is possible. But this should not mean that social workers could not support lay carers in the work they are doing to create narratives that work for them and those they support and which enable effective caring relationships. And if the role of social work in this context is primarily to act as co-ordinator of the various social care supports necessary to enable people to live in their own homes, then engaging with both life history narratives as well as constructive and re-constructive narratives is necessary to ensuring this range of support is delivered in line with the moral principles of attentiveness, responsibility, competence and responsiveness.

Conclusion

My rather ambitious objective in this book has been to propose and apply a framework which is relevant to the lived experience of care-givers and those they support, to the practices of those paid to help both care-givers and care-receivers, and which is also relevant to an understanding of the contribution of care to the achievement of social justice. In conclusion I want to contrast this with the way in which care is conceptualised within policy discourses. To illustrate I refer to the key policy document setting out UK government policy for carers: *Caring about Carers* (Department of Health, 1999).

Other commentators (Henderson and Forbat, 2002; Lloyd, 2000) have noted the absence of any developed understanding of care as a relational concept or practice within this text. There are brief references to ensuring that the 'empowerment' of carers does not result in detriment to the rights of care-receivers, including a specific acknowledgement that alternative support provided to enable carers to take a break should be experienced positively by the care-receiver as well as the carer. But the only reference to supporting carers and care-receivers' ability to do things *together* is in the context of taking holidays together. An all-pervading emphasis on the carer as a separate individual, distinct from those they care for, means there is little emphasis in the text on supporting care-givers and care-receivers jointly to engage in social, political, cultural or leisure pursuits. Nor is there explicit recognition of caring as a practice which takes place *through* relationships, rather than arising *from* a relationship. In this text carers are distinct from care-receivers and it is clear which is which, because care-receivers are the more needy of the two.

Through the use of a number of rhetorical devices, carers are distinguished as 'other': 'We need now to care about carers', 'Carers should not be pitied, but respected and admired' (p. 83). In this way, in spite of Tony Blair's introduction that appeals to readers to recognise care-giving as something that will be familiar to us all, caring is in fact separated and distanced from 'us'. If 'we' care about 'carers' then we do not need to care directly ourselves. Carers are set apart, perhaps placed on a pedestal where there is little room for the rest of 'us'.

We can summarise the discourse of care evident within *Caring about Carers* and other official policy regarding care as comprising the following:

- The care-giver is distinct from care-receiver who is needy and dependent.
- Care is a natural part of familial relationships.
- In particular, caring is a natural aspect of women's identities.
- Lay care is better than paid care.
- Care is a burden so those who provide it deserve the gratitude of society and relief from their responsibilities from time to time.
- Care takes place in the private sphere. This means that it is not considered an expression of citizenship, nor are the moral principles of care relevant to the construction of social policies which are concerned with the way in which we live together within communities.

In contrast the ethic of care discourse can be summarised in the following way:

- Care giving and receiving are part of the same process.
- We can all be both care-providers and care-receivers – at the same time or at different times in our lives.
- Care has to be worked at to be good care, but what constitutes 'good care' is not fundamentally different whether it is paid for or provided by family or friends.
- Care is an essential element of all human relationships in the public as well as the private sphere.
- Care-giving is an expression of citizenship and thus carries social rights equivalent to those accruing from employment.

The dominant overarching narrative of care-giving has become one of tragic heroine and needy client. I argue that a rather different metanarrative of caring is necessary to reflect what caring means to those involved in caring relationships and to overcome a perceived dichotomy between care and justice. People are not unconstrained in their capacities to create new narratives within which to live their lives. They live within a world in which assumptions and expectations about roles and possibilities are shaped both by dominant norms and by social structures. 'Not caring' was not an option for the carers whose stories I have told in this book and for the majority of those who support disabled, ill or frail friends or relatives. A wholesale shift from family and other forms of lay care to collective care or to care provided through market-place transactions is unlikely to take place and many would regard such shifts as undesirable. The challenge in this context is to develop policies and practices which value care and support it, but do not create a fixed identity of carer as either over-burdened drudge or tragic heroine.

The stories of care-giving told to me and summarised in this book do not underplay the hard work involved in caring, nor the way in which this has profound impacts on the lives of carers and on their relationships with those they care for. But they also suggest an 'ordinary life' narrative of care-giving: caring as a usual part of living together, interwoven with other family relationships, joys and tragedies, with personal aspirations and struggles, with work, with play and negotiating one's place in a social world structured by normative expectations of gendered family roles. They suggest that caring is something that needs to be directed at oneself as well as outwards to others, and that at different stages of life everyone is likely to be either/both care-giver and care-receiver. And they suggest that care-giving can be an important means through which people can, both individually and collectively, become active agents influencing and shaping the social world as well as building their own skills and confidence in their own capacity.

At an individual level it is important that practitioners recognise and work with this ordinary life narrative rather than that of the more dominant heroine and burden discourse. This is more likely to ensure a service response which recognises the relational dynamics of caring and which can deliver justice for both carer-givers and care-receivers. But such practices also need to be located within social policies that recognise the broader significance of care in social relationships. We need policies that support carers and those they care for, but we also need policies that support the value of care itself as a positive contribution to social justice. This will not be achieved as long as care-giving is understood as relevant only to those who are very young, old, ill or disabled.

References

Abrams, P. (1978) *Neighbourhood Care and Social Policy*, Berkhamsted: Volunteer Centre.

Aldridge, J. and Becker, S. (1994) *My Child, My Carer: The Parent's Perspective*, Loughborough: Young Carers Research Group, Department of Social Sciences, Loughborough University.

Altman, D. (1994) *Power and Community: Organizational and Cultural Responses to AIDS*, London: Taylor and Francis.

Alvesson, M. and Sköldberg, K. (2000) *Reflexive Methodology: New Vistas for Qualitative Research*, London: Sage.

Atkin, K. and Rollings, J. (1992) 'Informal care in Asian and Afro/Caribbean communities: a literature review', *British Journal of Social Work*, 22: 405–18.

Banks, S. (2001) *Ethics and Values in Social Work*, 2nd edition, Basingstoke: Palgrave.

Barker, P., Campbell, P. and Davidson, B. (eds) (1999) *From the Ashes of Experience: Reflections on Madness, Survival and Growth*, London: Whurr.

Barnes, C. (1991) *Disabled People in Britain and Discrimination: A Case for Anti-Discrimination Legislation*, London: Hurst.

Barnes, M. (1997a) *Care, Communities and Citizens*, Harlow: Addison Wesley.

Barnes, M. (1997b) 'Families and empowerment' in P. Ramcharan *et al.* (eds) *Empowerment in Everyday Life: Learning Disability*, London: Jessica Kingsley.

Barnes, M. (2001) 'From private carer to public actor: the Carers' Movement in England' in M. Daly (ed.) *Care Work: The Quest for Security*, ILO: Geneva.

Barnes, M. (2002a) 'Voices of users and carers – towards a new social movement?' Seminar in the Faculties of Sociology and Social Work, University of Trento, in memory of Alberto Melucci, May.

Barnes, M. (2002b) 'Bringing difference into deliberation: disabled people, survivors and local governance', *Policy and Politics*, 30 (3): 355–68.

Barnes, M. (2004) 'Affect, anecdote and diverse debates: user challenges to scientific rationality' in S. Harrison and A. Gray (eds) *Governing Medicine: Theory, Practice and Prospects*, Maidenhead: McGraw Hill/Open University Press.

Barnes, M. and Prior, D. (2000) *Private Lives as Public Policy*, Birmingham: Venture.

Barnes, M., Knops, A., Newman, J. and Sullivan, H. (2004) 'The micro politics of deliberation', *Contemporary Politics*, 10 (2): 93–110.

Bauman, Z. (2001) *The Individualized Society*, Cambridge: Polity.

Bayley, M. (1973) *Mental Handicap and Community Care*, London: Routledge and Kegan Paul.

Beck, U. and Beck-Gernsheim, E. (2002) *Individualization*, London: Sage.

Becker, S. (ed.) (1995) *Young Carers in Europe: An Exploratory Cross-National Study in Britain, France, Sweden and Germany*, Young Carers Research Group, Department of Social Sciences, Loughborough University.

Blunkett, D. (2003a) *Civil Renewal: A New Agenda*, CSV Edith Kahn Memorial Lecture, 11 June, London: Home Office /CSV.

Blunkett, D. (2003b) *Active Citizens, Strong Communities: Progressing Civil Renewal*, London: Home Office.

Bond, J. (1992) 'The politics of caregiving: the professionalisation of informal care', *Ageing and Society*, 12: 5–21.

Booth, T. and Booth, W. (1994) *Parenting Under Pressure*, Buckingham: Open University Press.

Borj, B. (2001) 'Child care as public policy in Brazil' in M. Daly (ed.) *Care Work: The Quest for Security*, Geneva: ILO.

Bornat, J., Dimmock, B., Jones, D. and Peace, S. (2000) 'Researching the implications of family change for older people: the contribution of a life-history approach' in P. Chamberlayne, J. Bornat and T. Wengraf (eds) *The Turn to Biographical Methods in Social Science*, London and New York: Routledge.

Bowers, B. J. (1987) 'Inter-generational caregiving: adult caregivers and their ageing parents', *Advances in Nursing Science*, 9 (2): 20–31.

Braithwaite, V. A. (1990) *Bound to Care*, Sydney: Allen and Unwin.

Brannelly, P. M. (2004) 'Citizenship and Care for People with Dementia', PhD thesis, School of Health Sciences, University of Birmingham.

Brechin, A., Barton, R. and Stein, J. (2003) 'Getting to grips with poor care' in K. Stalker (ed.) *Reconceptualising Work with Carers, New Directions for Policy and Practice*, London: Jessica Kingsley.

Briggs, A. and Oliver, J. (1985) *Caring: Experiences of Looking After Disabled Relatives*, London: Routledge and Kegan Paul.

Cameron, D. (2001) *Working with Spoken Discourse*, London: Sage.

Campbell, J. and Oliver, M. (1996) *Disability Politics: Understanding our Past, Changing our Future*, London: Routledge.

Caplan, P. (1985) *Class and Gender in India: Women and their Organizations in a South Indian City*, London and New York: Tavistock.

Chamba, R., Ahmad, W., Hirst, M., Lawton, D. and Beresford, B. (1999) *On the Edge: Minority Ethnic Families Caring for a Severely Disabled Child*, Bristol: Policy.

Chamberlayne, P. and King, A. (2000) *Cultures of Care: Biographies of Carers in Britain and the two Germanies*, Bristol: Policy.

Chamberlin, J. (1988) *On Our Own*, London: MIND.

Church, K. (1996) 'Beyond "bad manners": the power relations of "consumer participation" in Ontario's Community Mental Health System', *Canadian Journal of Community Mental Health*, 15 (2): 27–44.

Clarke, L. (1995) 'Family care and changing family structure: bad news for elderly people?' in I. Allen and E. Perkins (eds) *The Future of Family Care for Elderly People*, London: HMSO.

Collins-Hughes, E. (2001) 'Caring for carers: an example from Ireland' in M. Daly (ed.) *Care Work: The Quest for Security*, Geneva: ILO.

Crisp, J. (1999) 'Towards a partnership in maintaining personhood' in T. Adams and L. Clarke (eds) *Dementia Care: Developing Partnerships in Practice*, London: Ballière Tindall.

Curran, S. R. (2002) 'Agency, accountability and embedded relations: "What's love got to do with it?" ' *Journal of Marriage and Family*, 64 (August): 577–84.

Dalley, G. (1988) *Ideologies of Caring*, Basingstoke: Macmillan.

Daly, M. (2001) 'Care policies in Western Europe' in M. Daly (ed.) *Care Work: The Quest for Security*, Geneva: ILO.

Davis, A., Ellis, K. and Rummery, K. (1997) *Access to Assessment: Perspectives of Practitioners, Disabled People and Carers*, Bristol: Policy Press and Joseph Rowntree Foundation.

Department of Health (1997) *Health Action Zones – Invitation to Bid*, EL (97) 65, 30, October.

Department of Health (1999) *Caring About Carers*, London: Stationery Office.

Desmond, C., Michael, K. and Gow, J. (n.d.) *The Hidden Battle: HIV/AIDS in the Family and Community*, Durban: Health Economics and HIV/AIDS Research Division (HEARD), University of Natal.

Dixon-Fyle, K. (2002) *Social Policy with Respect to Care: A Perspective for Sub-Saharan Africa*, Geneva: SES Papers, International Labour Office.

Dominelli, L. (2002) *Anti-Oppressive Social Work: Theory and Practice*, Basingstoke: Palgrave.

Dooghe, G. (1992) 'Informal caregivers of elderly people: an European review', *Ageing and Society*, 12: 369–80.

Ehrenreich, B. and Hochschild, A. R. (eds) (2002) *Global Woman: Nannies, Maids and Sex Workers in the New Economy*, London: Granta.

Ellis, K. (1993) *Squaring the Circle*, York: Rowntree.

EOC (Equal Opportunities Commission) (1982) *Who Cares for the Carers? Opportunities for those Caring for the Elderly and Handicapped*, Manchester: EOC.

Etherington, K. (2000) *Narrative Approaches to Working with Adult Male Survivors of Child Sexual Abuse. The Clients' the Counsellors and the Researcher's Story*, London: Jessica Kingsley

Finch, J. (1984) 'Community care: developing non-sexist alternatives', *Critical Social Policy*, 9: 6–18.

Finch, J. and Groves, D. (eds) (1983) *A Labour of Love: Women, Work and Caring*, London: Routledge and Kegan Paul.

Finch, J. and Mason, J. (1993) *Negotiating Family Responsibilities*, London: Tavistock/Routledge.

Fisher, M. (1997) 'Older male carers and community care' in J. Bornat, J. Johnson, C. Pereira, D. Pilgrim and F. Williams (eds) *Community Care: A Reader*, 2nd edn, Basingstoke: Macmillan.

Folgerhaiter, F. (2004) *Relational Social Work: Towards Networking and Societal Practices*, London: Jessica Kingsley.

Fraser, N. (1997) *Justice Interruptus: Critical Reflections on the 'Postsocialist' Condition*, New York and London: Routledge.

Gibson, P. (2002) 'African American grandmothers as caregivers: answering the call to help their grandchildren', *Families in Society: Journal of Contemporary Human Services*, 83 (1): 35–43.

Giddens, A. (1998) *The Third Way: The Renewal of Social Democracy*, Cambridge: Polity.

Glasby, J. and Littlechild, R. (2002) *Social Work and Direct Payments*, Bristol: Policy.

Griffiths, R. (1988) *Community Care: Agenda for Action*, London: HMSO (Griffiths Report).

Gubrium, J. F. and Holstein, J. A. (1990) *What is Family?* Mountain View, CA: Mayfield.

Harber, M. (n.d.) *Social Policy Implications for the Care and Welfare of Children Affected by HIV/AIDS in KwaZulu-Natal*, Durban: Research Report no. 17, University of Natal, South Africa.

Harper, S. (1992) 'Caring for China's ageing population: the residential option – a case study of Shanghai', *Ageing and Society*, 12: 157–84.

Harrington Meyer, M. (ed.) (2000) *Care Work: Gender, Labor and the Welfare State*, New York: Routledge.

Harrington Meyer, M. and Kesterke Storbakken, M. (2000) 'Shifting the burden back to families?' in M. Harrington Meyer (ed.) (2000) *Care Work: Gender, Labor and the Welfare State*, New York: Routledge.

Harris, J. (2002) 'Caring for citizenship' *British Journal of Social Work*, 32 (3): 267–81.

Henderson, J. and Forbat, L. (2002) 'Relationship-based social policy: personal and policy constructions of "care"', *Critical Social Policy*, 22 (4): 669–87.

Hirst, M. (2001) 'Trends in informal care in Great Britain during the 1990s', *Health and Social Care in the Community*, 9 (6): 348–57.

Hochschild, A. R. (1983) *The Managed Heart: The Commercialisation of Human Feeling*, Berkeley: University of California Press.

Hondagneu-Sotelo, P. (2000) 'The international division of caring and cleaning work' in M. Harrington Meyer (ed.) *Care Work: Gender, Labor and the Welfare State*, New York: Routledge.

hooks, b. (1984) *Feminist Theory: From Margin to Center*, Boston, MA: South End.

James, N. (1992) 'Care=organisation+physical labour+emotional labour', *Sociology of Health and Illness*, 14 (4): 488–509.

James, S. M. (1993) 'Mothering: a possible black feminist link to social transformation?' in S. M. James and A. P. A. Busia (eds) *Theorising Black Feminisms*, London and New York: Routledge.

Jones, C. and Rupp, S. (2000) 'Understanding the carers' world: a biographical interpretive case study' in P. Chamberlayne, J. Bornat and T. Wengraf (eds) *The Turn to Biographical Methods in Social Science*, London: Routledge.

Jordan, B. (1989) *The Common Good: Citizenship, Morality and Self-Interest*, Oxford: Basil Blackwell.

Jordan, B. with Jordan, C. (2000) *Social Work and the Third Way: Tough Love as Social Policy*, London: Sage.

Katz, R. and Lowenstein, A. (2002) 'Family adaptation to chronic illness in a society in transition: the rural Arab community in Israel', *Families in Society: Journal of Contemporary Human Services*, 83 (1): 64–72.

Kitwood, T. and Bredin, K. (1992) 'Towards a theory of dementia care: personhood and well-being', *Ageing and Society*, 12: 269–87.

Labour Party (1997) *New Labour: Because Britain Deserves Better*, London: Labour Party.

Leibrich, J. (1999) *A Gift of Stories*, Dunedin: University of Otago Press.

Leira, A. (1990) 'Coping with care: mothers in a welfare state' in C. Ungerson (ed.) *Gender and Caring: Work and Welfare in Britain and Scandinavia*, Hemel Hempstead: Harvester Wheatsheaf.

Levin, E., Sinclair, I. and Gorbach, P. (1989) *Families, Services and Confusion in Old Age*, Avebury: National Institute for Social Work Research Unit.

Lewis, J. (1998) *Gender, Social Care and Welfare State Restructuring in Europe*, Aldershot: Ashgate.

Lewis, J. (2001) 'Legitimizing care work and the issue of gender equality' in M. Daly (ed.) *Care Work: The Quest for Security*, ILO: Geneva.

Lewis, J. and Meredith, B. (1988) *Daughters Who Care: Daughters Caring for Mothers at Home*, London: Routledge and Kegan Paul.

Lingsom, S. (1997) *The Substitution Issue*, Oslo: NOVA.

Lister, R. (1997) *Citizenship: Feminist Perspectives*, Basingstoke: Macmillan.

Lister, R., Smith, N., Middleton, S. and Cox, L. (2003) 'Young people talk about citizenship: empirical perspectives on theoretical debates', *Citizenship Studies*, 7 (2) 235–53.

Lloyd, L. (2000) 'Caring about carers: only half the picture?' *Critical Social Policy*, 20 (1): 36–57.

Lowndes, V. (2000) 'Women and social capital: a comment on Hall's 'Social capital in Britain', *British Journal of Political Science*, 30: 533–40.

Lund, F. (1991) 'Women, welfare and the community', paper presented at the conference on Women and Gender in Southern Africa, Centre for Social and Development Studies, University of Natal, Durban.

Mackay, F. (1998) 'In a different voice? Scottish women politicians and the vocabulary of care', *Contemporary Politics*, 4 (3): 259–70.

Marsh, P. and Fisher, M. (1992) *Good Intentions: Developing Partnership in Social Services*, York: Joseph Rowntree Foundation.

Mattingly, C. (1998) *Healing Dramas and Clinical Plots: The Narrative Structure of Experience*, Cambridge: Cambridge University Press.

Mayall, B. and Petrie, P. (1977) *Minder, Mother and Child*, London: Heinemann.

Mayo, M. (1994) *Communities and Caring: The Mixed Economy of Welfare*, Basingstoke: Macmillan.

Melucci, A. (1985) 'The symbolic challenge of contemporary movements', *Social Research*, 52 (4): 789–816.

Melucci, A. (1996) *Challenging Codes: Collective Action in the Information Age*, Cambridge: Cambridge University Press.

Middleton, D. and Hewitt, H. (2000) 'Biography and identity: life story work in transitions of care for people with profound learning difficulties' in P. Chamberlayne, J. Bornat and T. Wengraf (eds) *The Turn to Biographical Methods in Social Sciences*, London: Routledge.

Miller, R. L. (2000) *Researching Life Stories and Family Histories*, London: Sage.

Millett, K. (1991) *The Loony Bin Trip*, London: Virago.

Morris, J. (1995) 'Creating a space for absent voices: disabled women's experiences of receiving assistance with daily living activities', *Feminist Review*, 51: 68–93.

Morris, J. (2001) 'Impairment and disability: constructing an ethics of care that promotes human rights', *Hypatia*, 16 (4): 1–16.

Myles, S., Douglas, M. J., Ward, H. J. T., Campbell, H. and Will, R. G. (2002) 'Variant Creutzfeld-Jakob disease: costs borne by families', *Health and Social Care in the Community*, 10 (2): 91–8.

Nolan, M., Grant, G. and Keady, J. (1996) *Understanding Family Care*, Buckingham: Open University Press.

Ogg, J. and Bennett, G. (1992) 'Elder abuse in Britain', *BMJ*, 305 (October): 989–99.

Okely, J. (1999) 'Love, care and diagnosis' in T. Kohn and R. McKechnie (eds) *Extending the Boundaries of Care: Medical Ethics and Caring Practices*, Oxford and New York: Berg.

ONS (Office for National Statistics) (1998) *Annual Abstract of Statistics*, London: Government Actuary's Department.

Parker, G. (1985) *With Due Care and Attention: A Review of Research on Informal Care*, London: Family Policy Studies Centre.

Parker, G. (1993) *With this Body: Caring and Disability in Marriage*, Buckingham: Open University Press.

Parker, R. (1981) 'Tending and social policy' in E. M. Goldberg and S. Hatch (eds) *A New Look at the Personal Social Services*, London: Policy Studies Institute.

Parton, N. and O'Byrne, P. (2000) *Constructive Social Work: Towards a New Practice*, Basingstoke: Macmillan.

Pateman, C. (1992) 'Equality, difference, subordination: the politics of motherhood and women's citizenship' in G. Bock and S. James (eds) *Beyond Equality and Difference: Citizenship, Feminist Politics, Female Subjectivity*, London: Routledge.

Pattie, C., Seyd, P. and Whiteley, P. (2003) 'Citizenship and civic engagement: attitudes and behaviour', *Political Studies*, 51 (3): 443–68.

Penning, M. J. (2002) 'Hydra revisited: substituting formal for self- and informal in-home care among older adults with disabilities', *Gerontologist*, 42 (1): 4–16.

Pickard, S. and Glendinning, C. (2002) 'Comparing and contrasting the role of family carers and nurses in the domestic health care of frail older people', *Health and Social Care in the Community*, 10 (3) 144–50.

Pijl, M. (2000) 'Home care allowances: good for many but not for all', *Practice*, 12 (2): 55–65.

Pillemer, K. and Finkelhor, D. (1988) 'The prevalence of elder abuse: a random sample survey', *Gerontologist*, 28 (February): 51.

Putnam, R. D. (1993) *Making Democracy Work: Civic Traditions in Modern Italy*, Princeton: Princeton University Press.

Qureshi, H., Challis, D. and Davies, B. (1983) 'Motivations and rewards of helpers in the Kent Community Care Scheme' in S. Hatch (ed.) *Volunteers, Patterns, Meanings and Motives*, London: Policy Studies Institute.

Qureshi, H. and Walker, A. (1989) *The Caring Relationship: Elderly People and their Families*, Basingstoke: Macmillan.

Ramsay, R., Gerada, C., Mars, S. and Szmukler, G. (eds) (2001) *Mental Illness: A Handbook for Carers*, London: Jessica Kingsley.

Ray, M. (2000) 'Older women, long-term marriage and care' in M. Bernard (ed.) *Women Ageing: Changing Identities, Challenging Myths*, London: Routledge.

Richards, S. (2000): Bridging the divide: elders and the assessment process', *British Journal of Social Work*, 30: 37–49.

Rimmerman, C. A. (1998) *The New Citizenship: Unconventional Politics, Activism and Service*, Boulder, CO: Westview.

Sambisivan, U. (2001) 'Development, freedom and care: the case of India' in M. Daly (ed.) *Care Work: The Quest for Security*, Geneva: ILO.

Seidman, S. (1998) *Contested Knowledge: Social Theory in the Postmodern Era*, Oxford: Blackwell.

Settersten, R. A. (1999) *Lives in Time and Place: The Problems and Promises of Developmental Science*, Amityville, NY: Baywood.

SEU (Social Exclusion Unit) (2001) *A New Commitment to Neighbourhood Renewal: National Strategy Action Plan*, London: Cabinet Office.

Sevenhuijsen, S. (1998) *Citizenship and the Ethics of Care: Feminist Considerations of Justice, Morality and Politics*, New York and London: Routledge.

Sevenhuijsen, S. (2000) 'Caring in the third way: the relation between obligation, responsibility and care in *Third Way* discourse', *Critical Social Policy*, 20, (1): 5–37.

Shakespeare, T. (2000) *Help*, Birmingham: Venture.

Smale, G. and Tuson, N. (1993) *Empowerment, Assessment, Care Management and the Skilled Worker*, London: NISW/HMSO.

Social Services Inspectorate (1991) *Care Management and Assessment: Practitioners' Guide*, London: HMSO.

Stalker, K. (ed.) (2003) *Reconceptualising Work with Carers: New Directions for Policy and Practice*, London: Jessica Kingsley.

Standing, G. (2001) 'Care work: overcoming insecurity and neglect' in M. Daly (ed.) *Care Work: The Quest for Security*, Geneva: ILO.

Stone, D. (2000) 'Caring by the book' in M. Harrington Meyer (ed.) *Care Work: Gender, Labor and the Welfare State*, New York: Routledge.

Taccani, P. (ed.) (1994) *Dentro la Cura: Famiglie e anziani non autosufficienti*, Milan: FrancoAngeli.

Traustadottir, R. (2000) 'Disability reform and women's caring work' in M. Harrington Meyer (ed.) *Care Work. Gender, Labor and the Welfare State*, New York: Routledge.

Tronto, J. C. (1993) *Moral Boundaries: A Political Argument for an Ethic of Care*, New York and London: Routledge.

Tuominem, M. (2000) 'The conflicts of caring: gender, race, ethnicity and individualism in family child-care work' in M. Harrington Meyer (ed.) *Care Work. Gender, Labor and the Welfare State*, New York: Routledge.

Twigg, J. (1989) 'Models of carers: how do social care agencies conceptualise their relationship with informal carers?' *Journal of Social Policy*, 18(1) 53–66.

Twigg, J. (2000) *Bathing – the Body and Community Care*, London and New York: Routledge.

Twigg, J. and Atkin, K. (1994) *Carers Perceived: Policy and Practice in Informal Care*, Buckingham: Open University Press.

Twigg, J., Atkin, K. and Perring, C. (1990) *Carers and Services: A Review of Research*, London: HMSO.

Ungerson, C. (1987) *Policy is Personal. Sex, Gender and Informal Care*, London: Tavistock.

Ungerson, C. (1997) 'Give them the money: is cash a route to empowerment?' *Social Policy and Administration*, 31 (1): 45–53.

Van Gunsteren, H. R. (1998) *A Theory of Citizenship: Organizing Plurality in Contemporary Democracies*, Boulder, CO: Westview.

Vasey, S. (1996) 'The experience of care' in G. Hales (ed.) *Beyond Disability: Towards an Enabling Society*, London: Sage.

Walker, R. and Ahmad, W. (1994) 'Asian and black elders and community care: a survey of care providers', *New Community*, 20 (4): 635–46.

Waller, M. A. and Patterson, S. (2002) 'Natural helping and resilience in a Dine (Navajo) community', *Families in Society: Journal of Contemporary Human Services*, 83 (1): 73–84.

Walsh, J. (2001) 'Creating unions, creating employers: a Los Angeles home-care campaign' in M. Daly (ed.) *Care Work: The Quest for Security*, Geneva: ILO.

Warnes, A. M. (1997) 'Older people as social pioneers', thematic keynote highlights from the World Congress of Gerontology 'Ageing Beyond 2000: One World One Future' http://www.cas.flinders.edu.au/iag/proceedings/proc0034.htm

Warren, L. (1990) ' "We're home helps because we care": the experience of home helps caring for elderly people' in P. Abbott and G. Payne (eds) *New Directions in the Sociology of Health*, London: Falmer.

Wengraf, T. (2001) *Qualitative Research Interviewing*, London: Sage.

Whitehead, L. (2002) *Democratisation: Theory and Practice*, Oxford: Oxford University Press.

Williams, F. (2004) *Rethinking Families*, London: Calouste Gulbenkian Foundation.

Witcher, S., Stalker, K., Roadburg, M. and Jones, C. (2000) *Direct Payments: The Impact on Choice and Control for Disabled People'*, Edinburgh: Scottish Executive Central Research Unit.

Wood, R. (1991) 'Care of disabled people' in G. Dalley (ed.) *Disability and Social Policy*, London: Policy Studies Institute.

Young, I. M. (1990) *Justice and the Politics of Difference*, Princeton, NJ: Princeton University Press.

Young, I. M. (2000) *Inclusion and Democracy*, Oxford: Oxford University Press.

Index